Indian Art in America

INDIAN ART IN AMERICA

The Arts and Crafts of the North American Indian

FREDERICK J. DOCKSTADER

PROMONTORY PRESS · NEW YORK

This edition is published by arrangement
with the New York Graphic Society.

No part of this book, including any of the
illustrations, may be reproduced without
the written permission of the New York Graphic Society,
to whom all applications so to do should be adressed.

Library of Congress Catalog Card Number 73-89243
ISBN 0-88394-008-6

PRINTED IN HOLLAND

Printed by Smeets Lithographers, Weert
Design by Peter Oldenburg

Dedicated to the Memory of
FREDERIC H. DOUGLAS
A pioneer leader in the efforts to
establish an understanding
and appreciation of
the Indian and his arts

TABLE OF CONTENTS

Acknowledgments

In the preparation of a volume of this nature, the work of many people is involved. No one person can organize the myriad details, and I hasten to express my deep sense of obligation to those who contributed so fully to its completion:

To the Carnegie Foundation, and its Study of the Arts of the United States, directed by Dr. Lamar Dodd, of the University of Georgia. The patience and sympathetic consideration of Mr. William H. Pierson, Jr., and Mr. Charles B. Phelps of the Carnegie Study staff were of considerable assistance in organizing that portion of the work;

Mr. Herbert Schutz and Mr. Burton Cumming of the New York Graphic Society, without whose enthusiastic push and confidence this book would not have evolved;

Mr. Vincent Price, who perhaps more than any other individual gave the volume the necessary initial impetus;

Mr. Ralph C. Altman, whose many helpful suggestions have been incorporated into the text material;

Mrs. Jeanne Snodgrass, of the Philbrook Art Center, whose co-operation in the organization of the material on water color paintings was indispensable and enthusiastic;

Miss A. Frances Eyman, Assistant Curator at the University Museum, for her several contributions of information and suggestions;

and among other friends who unknowingly helped in so many ways are Dr. Robert T. Hatt, Mr. and Mrs. James A. Beresford, and Miss Emma Lila Fundaburk.

For the use of material and data included in this volume I am happy to acknowledge with sincere appreciation the courtesies of these individuals and institutions:

Dr. Harry Shapiro, Chairman, Anthropology Department, and the American Museum of Natural History, New York;

Dr. Robert T. Hatt, Director, and the Cranbrook Institute of Science, Bloomfield Hills, Michigan;

Dr. Froelich Rainey, Director, and the University Museum, Philadelphia, Pennsylvania;

Dr. Clifford Gregg, Director, and the Chicago Natural History Museum, Chicago, Illinois;

Dr. J. O. Brew, Director, and the Peabody Museum, Harvard University, Cambridge, Massachusetts;

Dr. Linton Satterthwaite, Curator, the University Museum, Philadelphia, Pennsylvania;

Dr. Paul S. Martin, Chairman, Anthropology Department, Chicago Natural History Museum;

Dr. Erna Gunther, Director, and the Washington State Museum, Seattle, Washington;

Mr. Lee B. Malone, Director, and the Portland Art Museum, Portland, Oregon;

Dr. Raymond S. Baby, Curator, and the Ohio State Museum, Columbus, Ohio;

Dr. Saul Reisenberg, Curator of Ethnology, and the United States National Museum, Washington, D.C.;

Miss Jane Powell, Curator of Primitive Art, and the Brooklyn Museum of Art, Brooklyn, New York;

Dr. Emil W. Haury, Director, and the Arizona State Museum, Tucson, Arizona;

Dr. M. R. Harrington, Curator, and the Southwest Museum, Los Angeles, California;

Dr. Robert Goldwater, Director, and the Museum of Primitive Art, New York City;

Dr. Stephen Borhegyi, Director, and the Stovall Museum, University of Oklahoma, Norman, Oklahoma;

Dr. T. M. N. Lewis, and the University of Tennessee, Knoxville, Tennessee;

Dr. James O. Swauger, Assistant Director, and the Carnegie Museum, Pittsburgh, Pennsylvania;

Dr. Donald T. Humphrey, Art Director, and the Philbrook Art Center, Tulsa, Oklahoma;

Mr. J. Edward Davis, General Manager, U.S. Indian Arts and Crafts Board, Washington, D.C.;

and to those many individuals who helped me so considerably by handling materials, supplying information, and performing in general the regrettably anonymous key services connected with such a task.

To Mr. E. K. Burnett, Director Emeritus, Museum of the American Indian, Heye Foundation, I extend my appreciation for his encouragement and patience during the preparation of this volume, Mr. William F. Stiles, Curator of that institution, was always ready to aid in the use of specimens from the museum's collections, and to share his knowledge about them.

I would be particularly remiss if I did not give special acknowledgment to two participants in the preparation of this book. A major proportion of the photographs were taken by Mr. Carmelo Guadagno, staff photographer of the Museum of the American Indian. His enthusiasm, talent, and meticulous attention to detail are evident in every illustration he provided. Even more appreciated was his willingness to do much more than was asked of him in giving this project his careful attention. And lastly, but certainly the influence which should head this list, my wife, Alice W. Dockstader, who took time from an overwhelming architectural responsibility to make suggestions, offer criticisms, and see to it that I did not stray too far from the typewriter.

Frederick J. Dockstader, *Director*
Museum of the American Indian
Heye Foundation

LIST OF ILLUSTRATIONS

II. *The Historic Period*

PLATE		PLACE OF ORIGIN
68	Carved human effigy figure of ivory	*Eskimo*
69	Carved ivory drum handle	*Eskimo*
70	Russian-style ivory pipe	*Eskimo*
71	Ivory shaman's doll with copper inlay	*Eskimo*
72	Wooden mask of "Up River Person"	*Ingalik*
73	Carved wooden spirit mask	*Eskimo*
74	Wooden dance mask of *Walaunuk*	*Eskimo*
75	Mask depicting a wolf and a seal	*Eskimo*
76	Wooden dance mask of *Negakfok*	*Eskimo*
77	Dance mask representing a seal	*Eskimo*
78	Fur parka and boots	*Eskimo*
79	Wooden *inua* mask; the seal and its spirit	*Eskimo*
80	Mother-and-child figurine	*Haida(?)*
81	The Land Otter Man	*Tlingit*
82	Carved and painted raven rattle	*Haida*
83	Carved wooden figurine of a woman	*Haida*
84	Carved wooden rattle; a beaver	*Kitksan*
85	Mask representing "The Mouse Man"	*Tlingit*
86	Wooden mask depicting the Brown Bear	*Tlingit*
87	Carved wooden mask of the Frog Spirit	*Tlingit*
88	Inlaid wooden mask; woman and frog	*Tlingit*
89	Carved bear-paw rattle	*Tlingit*
90	Mask of *Xoéexoae,* the bird-man spirit	*Kwakiutl*
91	Carved wooden movable mask; closed	*Kwakiutl*
92	Wooden mask of The Octopus Man	*Kwakiutl*
93	Mask of an old woman, with inlaid labret	*Niska*
94	Carved wooden movable mask; open	*Kwakiutl*
95	Mask depicting a poor woman	*Niska*
96	Double-face mask; the cannibal spirit	*Niska*
97	Wooden *Hámatsa* Society mask; wolf and skull	*Kwakiutl*
98	Carved wood fish-killing club	*Tlingit*
99	Carved antler "slave killer" club	*Haida*
100	Carved wooden spirit mask	*Tsimshian*
101	Carved wooden box drum	*Tlingit*
102	Carved wooden fish-killing club	*Haida*
103	Carved and painted house post	*Tlingit*
104	Wooden pipe bowl; eagle design	*Tlingit*
105	Carved whalebone club	*Kwakiutl*
106	Carved wooden pipe bowl	*Tlingit*
107	Carved wooden comb	*Tlingit*
108	Argillite carving; men in a boat	*Haida*
109	Ornamental carving of maple wood	*Tlingit*
110	Argillite carving; "Birth of the Bear Child"	*Haida*
111	Elaborate pipe of carved argillite	*Haida*
112	Wooden crest helmet; "The Noble Killer"	*Tlingit*
113	Argillite carving; "The Bear Mother"	*Haida*
114	Painted basketry hat	*Tlingit*
115	Argillite carving of a male figure	*Haida*
116	Carved wooden spoon	*Tlingit*
117	Ivory killer-whale charm; shell inlay	*Kitksan*
118	Ivory "soul catcher" with shell inlay	*Kitksan*
119	Carved ivory shaman's charms (2)	*Tlingit*
120	Carved ivory shaman's charms (3)	*Tlingit*
121	Hammered copper mask; The Mosquito	*Tlingit*
122	Inlaid ivory pipe of squatting figure	*Tlingit*
123	Hammered and painted "copper"	*Tlingit (?)*
124	Hammered copper rattle: shell inlay	*Tlingit*
125	Metal fighting knives (3)	*Tlingit*
126	Dance kilt; button design	*Haida*
127	Painted buckskin dance apron	*Tlingit*
128	Man's woven "Chilkat shirt"	*Tlingit*
129	Woven "Chilkat blanket"	*Tlingit*
130	Carved wooden movable figurine	*Nootka*
131	Carved wood mask	*Makah*
132	Wooden figure on a shaman's staff	*Quinault*
133	Carved figure of woman with cradle	*Songish*
134	Carved bird-handle adze	*Quileute*
135	Carved and painted *Swaixwe* mask	*Cowichan*
136	Carved wooden *Tamanus* board	*Salish*
137	Carved horn ladle	*Wasco*
138	Incised *Swaixwe* horn rattle	*Salish*
139	Woven container; human figure design	*Wasco*
140	Bark box with scraped design	*Montagnais*
141	Elkskin pouch with quilled decoration	*Chipewyan*
142	Quill-decorated knife sheath	*Chipewyan*
143	Basket with polychrome design	*Panamint*
144	Painted buckskin legging	*Naskapi*
145	Polychrome woven basket	*Chemehuevi*
146	Fern basket with dyed quill decoration	*Karok*
147	Basketry gambling tray	*Yokuts*
148	Polychrome basket, by Datsolali	*Washo*
149	Human effigy vessel of pottery	*Mohave*
150	Incised elk-antler purse	*Hupa*
151	Oval basket with beaded decoration	*Pomo*
152	Feather-decorated gift basket	*Pomo*
153	Painted pottery figurines	*Yuma*
154	Polychrome pottery fetish jar	*Zuñi*
155	Pottery jar with all-over deer design	*Zuñi*
156	Polychrome pottery water jar	*Acoma*
157	Polychrome pottery bowl	*Hopi*

PREFACE

The various manifestations of the artistic impulse of the American Indian are so limitless and complex that no one volume can hope to do the subject justice. This book is an attempt to gather together a general selection of some of the finest examples of North American Indian art, together with some specimens of everyday craftsmanship which possess unusual aesthetic qualities. The Indian arts of Mexico and Latin American areas have been excluded, for they are essentially quite different, and deserve completely separate treatment.

It has not been possible to represent all art styles and tribal groups; rather, the goal has been to include every important region, most of the numerically or artistically pre-eminent tribes, and all the major techniques employed by Indian artists. Certain unavoidable imbalances result from this manner of presentation, as well as from other factors. The Indian artist achieved a mastery of sculptural techniques in particular, and the selections are perhaps weighted heavily in that direction. Although there was certainly equal competence in other techniques, function or material restricted the artist's freedom of expression, and fewer "masterpieces" resulted. Some art was created in perishable materials, and there are so few specimens extant that it is impossible truly to assess the degree of artistry involved. Lastly, some work cannot easily be reproduced: sand paintings, for example, were created for specific ceremonies by sprinkling colored sands upon a prepared earth surface, then destroyed when the ritual had ended.

But a far graver matter is the treatment of the arts as such, for this study is limited to the visual arts of the Indian. It must be emphasized that the literature, poetry, music, and dance of the American Indian comprise a great part of his total art expression, and that some of his major potential contributions to American life lie in these fields. Regrettably, we have had to exclude these facets of his culture, with only portions of costume paraphernalia receiving fair attention.

It is hoped that the reader will gain an understanding of what had been done before the white man came—and what has happened to that art since. The effort will be made to present these examples somewhat as seen through Indian eyes, and thereby to interpret insofar as it is humanly possible the aesthetic and ethnological qualities of the object which would have importance in the Indian's thinking. There is no thought of investigating the deep psychological ramifications of human art expression in this volume, nor is it the writer's intention to attempt to analyze Indian character and thought through his art expression. This is much better left to the analytical psychologist, or perhaps to the more imaginative social anthropologist.

This book originally grew out of a project undertaken by the Carnegie Foundation, which in 1955 established the Carnegie Study of the Arts of the United States, under the direction of Dr. Lamar Dodd, of the University of Georgia. The author was privileged to serve as the Consultant on the Arts of the American Indian for that project, and the Carnegie collection forms the nucleus of this volume. That collection was chosen only from public museums in the United States, since the availability of the subjects for visual education use was a major factor in their selection.

Additions to this basic Carnegie collection have given this present work a greater balance, particularly in regard to the work of Canadian Indians. Circumstances make it impossible to canvass the entire North American continent for specimens. To the reader must be left some of the thrill of aesthetic exploration, for many museums possess treasures of equal aesthetic merit. The connoisseur may miss certain favorites or classic examples which have not been included for various reasons; but any selection is arbitrary, and it is hoped that he will encounter a sufficient number of other masterpieces so that he will not begrudge the loss.

Each specimen is presented in its most effective visual form (but without photographic tricks), together with adequate ethnographical information to enable the viewer to understand its use and origin. Its emotional or artistic appeal is a subjective matter, which the reader can best judge for himself. The sources of the articles illustrated are also given in the individual cap-tions; they came from the many fine collections throughout the country, albeit the majority are in museums easth of the Mississippi. Due to circumstances connected with the initial development of the Carnegie study, the bulk of the specimens came from the great collections of the Museum of the American Indian, Heye Foundation.

Most of the illustrations in this volume have never before been published; in providing this debut for many heretofore unknown Indian art objects, it is the author's hope that this volume will make Americans more familiar with a part of their heritage of which they may justly be proud. Perhaps they may also be inspired to explore that heritage more fully.

Introduction

THE INDIAN AS AN ARTIST

In any discussion of the art of the American Indian, or to achieve an understanding of what it represents, it is imperative that many preconceptions and judgments based on an evaluation of European art must be thrown out. A majority of the rules taught in art appreciation classes do not apply; indeed, the common ground of aesthetics does not always hold, simply because the two art forms are inevitably judged from differing points of view. An art critic seeking to utilize European ground rules in judging Indian art is bound to be unsuccessful. Applied by sympathetic viewers, they are only partially valid; in hostile hands, they are even less adequate.

Many devotees of the aboriginal arts believe that there are eternal truths which can be found in all cultures, and that to the sensitive eye, these aesthetic verities are independent of the cultural milieu involved. While this is true to a very limited extent, it is more important to remember that there are just as many differing standards which are applied by the native critic, and that many of these standards may be directly opposed to the opinions of the cosmopolite. This same-yet-different character must be grasped before a true understanding

Montezuma's Castle. The best-preserved archaeological ruin in the Southwest, this famed structure provides an excellent example of Pueblo architecture of the period. The need for security from marauders coupled with the natural skill of the designers produced a dwelling very similar to the castles being built in Europe at the same time.

Yavapai County, Arizona   1300–1500

can develop. The basic role of the artist is the same in any culture: to arouse an emotional response in his audience. If he fails to do so, then to that audience, he is not an artist. His failure may or may not be personal, for often the audience itself is at fault. The Indian artist's ability successfully to communicate with his own people depended on his recognition of the force of tradition. The social organization of the various tribes allowed less latitude for experimentation, and usually forced his work into well-known and widely understood channels. Yet along with this rigidity, there was sometimes a surprising degree of free expression.

The Indian artist's failure to reach a white audience is often due to the method of communication. In this instance *communication* means language in the broadest sense; it is not just a matter of linguistics, but entails bridging cultural, racial, social, and political barriers which have generally proven almost insuperable.

Art has been with man since prehistoric times; although the forms were simple, the urge to create something of beauty seems always to have been present. His first stonework was crude, but as these celts, arrowpoints, and blades were perfected, fine differences developed; today we can characterize cultures by the degree of quality displayed in their stone-working (Plate 18). Many utilitarian points were more carefully chipped than function strictly dictated. A rough stone celt with a polished blade will work perfectly well, but some were lovingly worked to an almost mirrorlike surface. They remain utilitarian, yet beauty has been added (Plate 19).

Art is relative; a creation may not necessarily be the finest in order to be an art expression. Some of the examples in this volume are more aesthetically pleasing than others—yet all can justifiably be classed as art. Some tribes developed their art expressions more capably than others, due to environment, economics, temporal factors, or other influences. But it can be said with certainty that all tribes had some form of art expression.

Few Indian groups allowed art to become a major way of life, as happened in Europe. Indeed, some Indian languages possess no word in their vocabularies for *art* or *artist*. Yet others had professionals who spent their lives creating objects of beauty for wealthy patrons.

The aim of the Indian artist was not merely to establish a realistic record. He quickly realized that he could not draw a tree as perfectly as it was made by the Creator. So, with good sense, he did not try. Instead, he sought out the spirit, or essence, of the tree, and represented it in his drawing. It is this semi-magical character, so common in Indian art, which is difficult for non-Indians to comprehend. Carvings, paintings, or "realistic" portraits are not simply pictures *of* people or objects; they embody the essence of that particular subject as well. The illustration captures the soul of the object, and is, in a manner of speaking, a form of witchcraft. Thus the Indian used to avoid the photographer, because to him a photograph represented a capturing of his soul, and thereby weakened him. He believed that if his soul fell into evil hands, he became a prisoner; conversely, in good hands, it had the force of creativity and could produce beneficial results. In his art, a good spirit embodied in a reproduction would assure good fortune. Contemporary artists often follow a similar course, seeking graphically to represent emotions, spiritual essence, or unseen forces hidden behind a subject's physical façade. The art of painting visions or mental impressions is not new.

Ritual was often interwoven with the art of the Indian. For example, in European terms the Zuñi War God (Plate 174) is wood sculpture of a religious nature; such a definition would suffice, and other details would simply be added ethnographic information. To the Zuñi, however, it is vitally important that the wood come from a tree which has been struck by lightning, and that it be ritually prepared for carving. Or, again, the mask in Plate 233 was carved from the trunk of a living tree—hence the term "live mask." The tree was ritually addressed before the carver began, and the mask and tree were "fed" tobacco before separating the two.

Such ritual was of equal, if not greater, importance than the artistic skill employed in finishing the object. If the ritual were ignored, the article would lose its efficiency, and might even counteract any possible beneficial results. The ritual aspect of Indian art permeates a major part of the ceremonial paraphernalia, and is extremely complex. It involved the Indian's

entire world, and had to be considered every step of the way. To the Indian, such ritual was a vital and equal part of whatever he termed "art."

However, it must be emphasized that not all Indian artists were priests or magicians, nor was all their artwork religious in content; there was much that was humorous, profane, and mundane. Indeed, if there is any one truism in considering Indian cultures, it is that *there is no consistency.* Immediately a rule is established concerning an "accepted" way of doing something, an exception will be found. The Indian varied his themes, just as other tribes, races, or nations do, but all his art expressions represent a part of man's approach to a common aesthetic goal.

What Is Indian Art? This term covers an extremely broad category, encompassing all art expressions of the aborigines of America and their descendants. It includes not only many widely varied and disparate cultures, but also spans great time sequences. The only common bond held by these artists is their basic racial origin.

During the several chronological periods there were regional characteristics of style which can be separately recognized, and even here, pronounced tribal variations often developed. Throughout these periods, borrowing of art forms from distant and occasionally alien peoples was a common practice.

The historical continuity of regional art forms can be readily observed in historic periods; in prehistoric times this is less clearly traced. In examining such highly developed art forms as shown in Plates 21 to 30, we find a sophisticated art concept which seemingly sprang, full-flowered, into being, and then vanished overnight—leaving no obvious traces of ancestry or descendants. Such examples are not isolated, and they occur frequently in the prehistory of America. Where did these mystery people come from and where did they go? It may be that such a sudden disappearance of an art form was due to natural disaster; equally likely, tribal warfare, in which the victorious group imposed its own art upon the vanquished, levied its toll. Such eradication of a culture has frequently taken place in world history.

In historic times we can follow a tribal or regional style through its many ramifications to the contemporary modification without too great difficulty, particularly in the Southwest; in other regions more intensive research may be required. Often such an investigation reveals the imposition of an alien art form by the victorious majority; this is particularly true in North America. A lack of understanding by the white majority has tended to discourage the Indian artist from developing his talents, and erasure of the minority art expression from the contemporary scene is a very real possibility. The white patron has failed to recognize that Indian art should be a continuing, creative force, rather than a confined traditional form, and this failure has served to limit radically the vitality of the Indian. In time his art becomes reduced to a static copybook activity, in which all creativity is extinguished.

With the above in mind, let us examine some of the cataloguing problems which confront any student interested in the subject of Indian art.

Characteristics. Just what are the general qualities by which we recognize Indian art? How do we instinctively differentiate the art of North America from, say, that of Oceania, Africa, or perhaps the neighboring continent to the south?

Obviously, the materials used are important. The student can often determine at a glance where a given article originated simply by what it is made of. Thus the pouch in Plate 229 could come only from North America; no other peoples used porcupine quills in this manner.

The concept of the article is itself an important criterion. The way of making something may or may not be similar to other areas. While clubs are clubs throughout the world, only the Indian seems to have developed the particular club shape illustrated in Plate 208.

Color and design are often clues, but this can also be deceptive. Combinations such as those in Plates 147 or 152 would identify the articles as Amerindian to most students, whereas the polychrome basket in Plate 214 has parallels elsewhere.

By and large, Indian art is considered primarily two dimensional; yet this, too, has many exceptions, as a glance through this volume will quickly reveal. It is as often termed an *applied art,* since so much of the decoration is applied to a prepared surface, yet fully half the examples we include are expressed in other than applied terms.

The Indian artist usually demonstrates a magnificent appreciation of shapes and forms. When undecorated, as in Plates 17, 18, and 20, his work still shows the feeling for sheer form. Many of his utilitarian objects were fashioned with this consciously effected; in other instances, a natural form was elaborated on.

In designing for space, which was one of the major Indian problems, he was faced with a challenge quite different from that of his European counterpart. A European painter, for example, usually started with an artificial limitation—a rectangular surface, which could be embellished in any way he chose. The Indian rarely had squared edges on his canvas; he used a whole buffalo hide, sticks as they came from trees, or the stone as it was found.

He was less prone to force his material into his design, but more or less adapted to its natural outline. This freedom from rigidity is often one of the most pleasing aspects about Indian art, and some pieces demonstrate an astonishingly natural feeling because of the way the individual has incorporated the natural form into his composition.

Just what does the Indian artist try to accomplish, beyond evoking an emotion? Perhaps his first step toward art is the beautification of his immediate environment—his home, his clothing, and various personal possessions. The clay of his pottery presented a smooth surface to be painted, incised, modeled, or inlaid, as did the great wealth of wood, stone, or other materials. Each of these substances presented him with a challenge—and the illustrations in this book reveal how successfully he met it.

But the Indian artist attempted more than simple embellishment and the evocation of an emotional response. By soothing, pleasing, or frightening the beholder, whether a god or a person, he sought to control his environment and human or supernatural behavior.

Possessing a keen sense of humor, the artist also aroused laughter with his art—and sometimes at his own expense. Humor was no stranger to the Indian, and many of the examples of art displayed in museums and regarded with solemnity by both curator and viewer alike were originally intended simply for amusement.

Another completely human emotion, the erotic, is also part of this complex. Although the total percentage of erotic art in the whole of North American art is not high, there is much more than is commonly realized. Much of it has disappeared in the Puritan fires which continue to burn the white man, but sufficient examples remain to indicate a wholly natural freedom of expression and a healthy naturalism at work.

Regionalism. Indian art is a provincial expression. It can be catalogued into as many major areas as there are critics. Some say five, some, seven; we have chosen nine as being most readily discernible and separable from each other. In these nine there is a certain unity of approach and commonality of material and technique, but even these include many peripheral or aberrant forms. The divisions were largely determined by environmental or temporal factors, which were tremendously affected by migration and intercourse through trade.

The nine regions are listed and individually classified in the following pages, both by geographic area and by chronological division, and are located in the map on page 25. It should be understood that it is in the border areas that the overlapping and the diffusion of influences is most marked. It is often completely impossible to identify with certainty examples of Indian art which have been collected near the boundaries of the various regions.

An interesting aspect of this regionalism is that although most tribes made more or less the same basic articles, those from one area are usually quite different than the same articles from a distant section. Many peoples lived in sandy areas, and, indeed, the Pueblos seem to have worked with colored sand designs for many centuries—yet the Navajo developed this art to its greatest height. All tribes had dolls—why were the Hopi and Zuñi almost the only groups to produce such an elaborated art form in their Kachina dolls? Sometimes, too, tribes with similar resources utilized them differently. Although other folk had great forests, none but the Northwest Coast people developed the complex which gave rise to the carving of huge totem poles. Why this is so is best left to the psychologist, but the question raises itself throughout this study.

Functionalism. Indian art was made to do work. In later years there came into existence a body of articles meant simply to beautify, but earlier "art" objects had to perform a service, and only secondarily were intended to beautify. This was no reflection upon Indian sensitivity; these people traveled intensively, and everything they possessed had to provide a maximum of service. Only in the later, more sophisticated, years were they able to afford the luxury of household possessions which did nothing but "look nice."

Often the articles were designed to serve supernatural beings rather than man; for, as with all people, the best of Indian artwork was applied to those objects intended for a god. Many objects had a surprising duality: normally, they were used for everyday household purposes, yet under a different set of circumstances they had either religious or social functions. Some specific articles were reserved for religious use only, some were religious and secular, and some were for secular purposes only.

However, decoration does not always provide the clue. Some of the most highly revered religious articles are completely plain—actually, rather ugly; others are fantastically embellished. Some women used plain bowls for food preparation, while others did the same chore in lovely polychrome ware. The Indian is no different in his imponderables than a present-day housewife.

Religion in Art. Many objects served hidden purposes. Under one set of circumstances, they would have an everyday function; yet beneath the surface, a magic was at work. The vessel had the power to call upon unseen forces to aid the owner, or in initiated hands, a mundane article might release its stored-up power. One such is shown in Plate 154. This power might be expressed visually or symbolically, or might be suggested by the form, shape, or decoration. This magical quality is akin to religion, and is usually impossible to detect without prior knowledge.

The so-called "traditional" qualities of an Indian object are frequently simply custom which has become long established through time and use. Though no one understands the origins

the tradition persists through convenience, laziness, or perhaps fear of the consequences if it is ignored. Thus some art decorations are continued without the creator's really understanding why. Nor does he particularly care; it is pleasing to the eye, satisfying to the soul, and calming to the nerves. The Indian is not one to jeopardize the *status quo* in religious matters.

Environment. It must be remembered that Indian art is the only true native art of North America. As such, it is also perhaps the highest artistic expression of the American environment. The Pueblo farmer expressed an agricultural point of view in much of his artwork; the Eastern Woodlands carver regarded wood, from the lush forests, as truly *his* personal medium of expression; the Plainsman employed the ample resources of grasses and hides, performing his work with paint and quill. Their work revolved around and grew out of the natural resources provided by their Creator; in turning these resources into artistic objects, they return the compliment.

Materials, tools, and techniques reflect the environment, which the Indian artist utilized to the utmost. This ability to create art with the simplest ingredients is one of the striking qualities of Indian artwork. A glance through the illustrations in this volume immediately reveals many examples of fine art achieved with relatively crude tools applied to an everyday material. This characteristic accounts for the charm which Indian art, or any folk art, has for us today, and creates respect for the cultures producing it.

The Indian's inventive nature is best expressed in some of his highly ingenious mechanical processes, and also shows up in his ability to adapt. The Eskimo is particularly famed for this talent. Not only did most tribes immediately and profitably adopt new tools, but they also freely borrowed from neighboring groups.

To be sure, the environmental factor had some serious limitations. The desert-dweller could not use wood freely; hence he rarely excelled in wood carving. Just as the Eskimo is not known for his shellwork, neither is the Plains Indian famed for ceramics; the one lacked a suitable raw material at home, while the other lived a nomadic life which precluded the wide use of fragile containers. Some tribes overcame limitations in resources by trade: shellwork, for example, is known to have been a highly developed art, and a prized commodity, among peoples who lived a great distance from the shore line. Thus, while environmental barriers existed, the Indian did not allow them to strangle his art.

Techniques and Expressions. The subject of techniques and expressions will be considered under the various regional treatments which follow, but there are a few observations which are pertinent here. First, literally any and every natural material at hand has been employed by the Indian artist in one way or another, among them such improbable substances as milkweed fibers, cactus thorns, and isinglass. Second, of the great variety of techniques employed, all involved a rather considerable amount of labor. To the Indian artist, time was relatively unimportant. Eskimo artists whiled away long hours in intricate carving; many pastoral people used the time advantageously by fashioning fine art products, and during the off season, the farming folk had ample time elaborately to decorate their personal and ceremonial possessions.

The concern with detail may be responsible for the so-called *horror vacui* which so many people sense in Indian art expression. The desire to fill a blank space is seemingly irresistible to many artists, and not infrequently results in an unfortunate excess of decoration. It is not often that such thoroughly covered jars as the Zuñi water vessel in Plate 155 satisfactorily overcome the objection of undue detail. Indeed, its design is akin to other repeat-pattern motifs so common in Indian art, as shown in Plates 147 and 224; were it not for skillful use of color and design, these items would not be so attractive. But always the relief offered by such distinguished compositions as the mica hand, Plate 28, and the superb diorite bowl, Plate 61, attest to the value of restraint.

Folk Art and Fine Art. Indian art is, of course, folk art, yet it contains many examples of fine art; the individual object must speak for itself. Most Indian artists were not trained in the formal sense; yet some tribes trained artists who made their living by creating *objets d'art* for their kindred, or for outside sale.

In Indian terms, there is no quarrel of art versus craft—the one leads to the other; it is only with an artificial classification that such a decision becomes important. The difference can be defined in terms of quality: any craft object becomes a work of art when exceptional creativity is accompanied by exceptional technical skill.

Most of the skilled works presented in this volume demonstrate exceptional creativity as well as fine technique.

If training is regarded as a criterion, it must be pointed out that all too often the non-Indian critic ignores the fact that training of the traditional tribal variety can be as thorough and as profound as any formal learning gained in schools.

Craftwork in itself is not art. It may be, but it is primarily a technical expression in which skill dominates creativity. In European terms, the sculptor who creates a clay statue original may or may not carve it in marble. But if another person executes that design in marble, using the clay model as a guide, he is not considered an artist—but simply a skilled craftsman. The creative hand belongs to the true artist. And, with economic pressures, much of the Indian's recent work has degenerated into mere copying.

Tradition. The comment is frequently heard, "Oh! but that is not traditional Indian work." This is usually intended to mean that the article is not what the speaker regards as "old-time Indian art." What that speaker does not realize is that there is no such thing as traditional Indian art, and that the "tradition" may be no more than a few years old—and, in many instances, introduced from alien sources.

Two examples illustrate this point. There was no Navajo silversmithing before 1853, when the art developed out of contacts with Mexican ironsmiths and saddle-workers. Hence, "traditional Navajo silverwork" cannot be more than about one hundred years old. Secondly, the general style of water-color painting as we know it today stems largely from Indian School teaching developed in the 1920's. Hence, this "traditional style of Indian painting" cannot be more than a half-century old, at most, and some of the innovators are still living. Indeed, is it valid to call either of these truly "traditional Indian art," since both are relatively short-lived so far, and introduced by non-Indians at that?

The sources of the various art traditions are impossible to analyze in most respects. The older traditions have grown out of a combination of factors—principally time, practice, and environment. The examples cited above demonstrate that outside influence was also a factor. In the old days, this influence came from neighboring tribes; today, it is largely from white culture.

Undoubtedly the most important factor, however, is time. Over a period of centuries, methods of art expression became popular in given areas, and were accepted and used until they became established in the people's minds. The art activities of isolated tribes, cut off from outside influence, became rigid and ingrown, and were affected only by the infrequent intruder, trader, or by the development from within of a single gifted individual. But unless this creative person possessed a particularly strong personality, he was often overcome by the more powerful forces of tradition.

True tradition, then, should be regarded as that which custom has developed and handed down from one generation to another over a period of time, rather than the short-lived stylistic development which can come and go within a single generation. *Tradition* can only be used in referring to tribal art, never to the generic "Indian art" form.

Style. Along with the longer lasting concept of tradition is the limited one of style, which changes readily. An art style is a particular expression of the traditional art form—what might be called "a way of doing something"—the application of paint in set color combinations (lineal as against geometric design), a method of handling human figures; a set of proportions; line, shape, or any given combination of elements which make up an identifiable art expression. Although characteristics of style are oftentimes duplicated elsewhere, by and large they are sufficiently individualistic to enable an expert to identify in general terms the tribal origin of most subjects.

Tribal Identity. It is exceedingly difficult accurately to establish tribal provenience of an article, particularly since the Indian traded far and wide. This shattered integrity of style, for when the Indian carried new materials into distant lands, he brought new ideas; and he carried different ideas and materials back with him when he returned. Many of these ideas were visual stimuli—designs, decorations, and forms which he applied to his own articles. In time they became part of the style of his people and were incorporated into their own traditional art; and now they present the ethnologist with a pretty problem.

And it does not end there. Many tribes required their young people to marry outside the tribe. This meant that the girl (who was generally the artist) took her own art ideas to another group. In time, these often became part of the art style of the new group. As a result, it is often impossible to establish with certainty the given maker of an article unless one knows for sure where and under what circumstances it was made.

An example is the well-known "cornhusk bags" of the Northwest Plateau folk. Usually they are called Nez Percé bags, because this tribe was the source of the majority of them (Plates 185 and 186). Yet a twined container made by four or five neighboring tribes is so similar as to be essentially indistinguishable. These tribes all require their people to marry outside the immediate group—which means that usually the marriage is within this general cluster of Shahaptian-speaking, bag-making people.

Sex. In this connection, it is interesting to note the degree to which we judge the whole culture of a tribe by the work of its womenfolk. For much of the material culture of the American Indian is the product of feminine activity. True, the Hopi men wove, Plains men painted their ceremonial objects, and Iroquois men carved wooden utensils and masks; but I think it is far more significant that we tend to base much of our evaluation of the aboriginal culture of the Indian on pottery, basketry, beadwork, costuming, and so on—most of which was done by women. Any judgment of Indian artistry must consider the woman's contribution.

It seems reasonable to assume that much the same division of labor was customary in prehistoric times. Therefore, stonework must have been done by men—the flaking, chipping, grinding, and carving of stone statues, effigies, tools, utensils, and points. Since our archaeological theories are based largely upon stone evidence—the men's work—we evaluate pre-

historic cultures by one set of attitudes, and the historic, by another.

The participation of women as artists introduces the element of tribal prohibitions on the kind of work they may perform. In many tribes, the men handle all religious arts and the women, the secular activities. In such situations, no woman may make or use a religious artifact. In other cases, the taboo applies only to the manufacture, and the women may use certain religious articles which the men make. Only a few tribes allow women to make articles for religious function, which the men use—and these are usually pottery, textiles, or basketry, having also a secular function.

Occasionally this causes a peculiar diversity in the arts of a tribe. Plains painting on hide as done by women is shown in Plate 204; the style of hide painting done by Plains men is partially illustrated by Plate 211. The two are quite disparate, yet were made during the same period and come from the same region under the same set of circumstances.

The Artist's Role. Further, the artist may have a different function from one tribe to another, and perhaps from one chronological period to another. Sometimes the work is solely that of the women; sometimes, of the men. In some instances, anyone may be an artist; in others, the work is restricted to specific individuals who possess the proper talent, training, or religious background.

Indian groups did not permit individual expression as much as European cultures did. It was regarded as much better to develop a prescribed style or traditional design to its ultimate than to branch out into something totally new and unknown. This was partly due to the co-operative nature of Indian lifeways and partly to those of custom, forces which exerted both a religious and social pressure.

However, while this obligation to conform predominated, there have been individual expressions in recent times which have made considerable changes in the art and economy of their respective groups. Perhaps the most carefully recorded have been the careers of Nampeyó, the Hopi potter, and María and Julián Martínez of San Ildefonso. Through sheer individual talent each of these achieved a complete personal triumph by developing a style which not only was copied by other potters, but which in time came to be regarded as "traditional" in that particular village. Examples of their style are shown in Plates 157 and 159.

We have no way of knowing to what extent this has happened in the past. There is considerable evidence that it may have occurred at Mimbres, among the Haida slate carvers, and perhaps in some areas of the so-called Mound Builders of the Woodlands and Southeast. Regardless of the actual number of such artists of genius, it is clear that the strong individual was in a position to influence greatly the work of his people, in spite of the tendency toward conformity, which was undoubtedly also present in early times.

The professional artist was also a factor. It is not widely realized that talented artists who made a career, and a livelihood, out of their artistic ability comprised an elite group in a few Indian societies. In some instances, they produced religious paraphernalia and, in return, were supported by their tribesmen. In others, they made and sold products commercially—any who would pay (or barter) for the product could purchase it.

Among the Northwest Coast people, "stables" of such artists were retained by wealthy chiefs to turn out the huge quantities of wood carvings, totem poles, and utensils by which prestige was maintained. Raiding parties were careful to bring artists back alive, to serve as slaves and turn out the desired paraphernalia and artwork. This existence of slaves from alien tribes further confuses the problem of proper identification of tribal artifacts.

It was the professional artist who exercised the most profound influence upon his tribe's art traditions and styles before there was contact with the white man. Where he existed, he was the one who made careful studies of style, copied or discarded designs, abstracted patterns, and chose bits here and there until he was pleased with his experimentation. And from this came the new designs, styles, and expressions which were ultimately copied by his fellow craftsmen.

Sources of Indian Design. The origins of most of the decorative designs shown in this volume's illustrations cannot be accurately traced today; most of them are lost in antiquity. Many obviously came directly from natural forms, while others are simple developments of lineal or geometric motifs. Whole studies have been devoted to the possible origin and influences of such art elements as the so-called "double-curve motif" of the Eastern Algonquian folk (Plate 145), and the dot-and-circle motif of the Eskimo (Plate 3). These designs have such a confused origin, and are today so thoroughly intermixed, that only academic dissertations can deal with the problem. Some of them have revealed a relationship among these designs, a few of which have readily traced origins and extremely interesting histories. When the origin of a design is known, the information has been incorporated in the captions accompanying the illustrations in this book.

Of greater immediate interest is the fact that a majority of the religious and semi-religious motifs used in Indian art originated in the artist's dream world. To the Indian, the dream world was an unknown land of supernatural activity in which his soul left his body and participated in many strange activities. The individual would carefully recreate his dream design on hide, wood, canvas, or whatever; it was regarded as a gift from the supernatural beings which would give him guidance and protection in the earth world. Sometimes, as with Eskimo shamans, he would describe his dream creature, and the men of the village would make masks representing that being for use in the next festival (*see* Plate 74).

Visions are closely akin to dreams, and the difference between the two is perhaps only strictly technical. Many tribes, particularly in the Plains region, expected the young man to go out alone, fasting, into the country and seek a vision which would become part of his holy medicine, to guide him through life. This quest was usually one of the stages in life development, for the man might go on several. These were not always successful, and if he failed, he simply tried again. Such a vision, which was actually hallucinatory or self-hypnotic in nature, was used in art in just the same manner as was the dream.

Since these supernatural dream and vision designs were extremely personal, most of them were applied by the individual himself. Thus they vary tremendously in artistic skill, depending upon the ability of the individual, and include many examples whose interest is primarily ethnological. But some, especially those shown in Plates 196 and 197, are of considerable art value, as well as of academic interest; the design, use of color, and composition give ample evidence of notable aesthetic skill.

The alien origins of designs *via* trade routes, introduction of new materials or motifs, and intermarriage have been mentioned. A design could also be bought from its creator, or it might be "given" to another artist. This was possible because the tribe regarded designs as personal property, and its members respected the artist's right to control or dispose of them, much as copyrighted material is today.

Realism. Generally the Indian artist's aim was to make a realistic record. The ability to achieve it varied from tribe to tribe, from artist to artist. Sometimes the preferred art style worked against true realism, sometimes it helped it. However, what is real to one group may be completely unreal to another—particularly when the tools available impose limitations on the artist. The stone art of the prehistoric Southeast provides samples of this problem (Plate 41); a considerable degree of realism is expressed, yet perfection has not been attained.

Sometimes it is difficult to know whether the artist intended a realistic portrait but lacked the necessary skill, or whether he deliberately avoided a direct likeness. Furthermore, many artists attempt to portray supernatural elements "realistically." To the uninitiated, the representation might appear wholly unreal, yet to the artist, it would be a completely truthful image: to him it is real, not imaginative.

Abstract. The Indian artist is the abstractionist *par excellence*, yet the abstract art of the Northwest Coast and the Southwest has affected the modern art movement but slightly. Examples of his ability to abstract elements from the whole and express them in an original manner are shown in Plates 129 and 182. His skill at taking these abstracted elements and fitting them into given areas or confining spaces is superb; and this talent is not limited to any one tribe, for it is common to many of the areas of aboriginal North America.

Symbolism. Of all phases of American Indian art, symbolism is the most widely misunderstood. It fascinates the average person to a tremendous degree, and the uninitiated is usually quite willing to believe anything he is told about the "meaning" of art designs. There are always self-appointed experts equally willing to supply those meanings. Frequently the Indian artist does express himself in symbols unintelligible to the white observer. But it should be pointed out immediately that much of this symbolism is equally unintelligible to other Indians, too!

Some abbreviated designs are a "secret code" which requires some initiation for comprehension. Such pieces as the birch-bark Midéwiwin Scrolls and song records (Plate 223) are meaningless to nonmembers, yet they have a definite meaning to Midé participants. Symbolic motifs may also have significance only to the artist or to his client, and may be unrelated to anything or anyone else in that culture. Sometimes a wife puts designs into her beadwork which represent some elements important in her husband's exploits (Plate 194); even he may not fully understand this unless she makes it perfectly clear to him how she interpreted his accomplishments in her work.

The artist's tendency to name designs also confuses the situation. When asked, an Indian will frequently call a given design a "leaf," or an "arrowhead," when what he actually means is that the design is "leaflike," or "leaf-shaped," or that it "looks like an arrowhead." The inquirer immediately translates this to mean that the design *signifies* a leaf or an arrowhead, and has difficulty unraveling any "story" in the combination of designs used.

In substance, it can be said that a majority of Indian decorative designs used on nonreligious objects have the same "meaning" to the Indian artist or layman as designs on clothing do to the ordinary housewife. When she ventures downtown in a flowered print dress, she is certainly not trying to relate the story of her back-yard flower garden. These are, to her, merely attractive designs and colors employed in an attractive manner; so she regards them, and so would her Indian counterpart.

To explain the steps from realism to symbolism more clearly, it might be well to present this example of Pueblo art:

REALISM   STYLIZED   ABSTRACT

SYMBOLIC   PETROGLYPH

It can be readily seen just how each of these have developed, the one out of the other. In context they are quite clear; but isolated and included with other abstract or symbolic designs the individual element would not be so obvious.

Commonality of Art. Some art students have advanced the suggestions that specific classes of articles result in great aesthetic achievements and that certain areas more or less automatically produce great masterpieces. Neither theory is entirely true, although each has enough accuracy to warrant consideration.

Firstly, it has been held that the art of mask-carving represents the ultimate in a tribe's aesthetic accomplishments, since masks are usually intended for serious religious purposes. Yet this can easily be contradicted: for example, the masks of the Naskapi are extremely crude in comparison to their elegant costume arts; or, to compare tribally, matching the work of the Cherokee, Iroquois, or Cochití mask-makers against that of the Tlingit, Tsimshian, or Niska mask-makers will immediately dispel any thought that the object *per se* dictates the quality of the art.

Furthermore, skill in one craft does not insure skill in all. Environment and material seem to have little close relationship to aesthetic heights. California basket-weavers produce some of the finest such containers in the world; yet their pottery, costuming, and other artifacts fall far short of this greatness. Specialization is a frequent occurrence. Nor does the use of any one material necessarily result in superfine work: wood can be a great art medium in the hands of a Tlingit carver, but not in those of a Plainsman.

Nor does location assure uniform artistic quality. The wood carving arts of the Northwest Coast are unquestionably superior, yet their costuming is much less artistically impressive than that of many neighboring regions. The Plains people, who excelled at the costume arts, were far less able in designing pottery and basketry.

One reason is that the purpose of various articles differs. Many of the masks mentioned above were intended to be grotesque or repulsive. Also, since some materials were scant in certain areas, many tribes felt little need for particular categories of art products. This is one more reminder that there is no such thing as Indian art—it is too varied an emotional expression.

The "Primitive Art" Concept. The flexibility and lack of homogeneity in Indian art rules out any attempt to classify it as primitive art, which is why the term has been avoided throughout this volume.

For example, it would be ridiculous to classify the paintings in Plates 188 and 218 as examples of primitive art. They are completely sophisticated expressions, both in content and technical execution. If *primitive* is to imply "primacy," then very little of this work can be such, for it is but the fruit of custom, practice, and teaching. If it is to denote "less than well done," this, too, clearly does not apply; few non-Indian artists could do as well.

Nor can *primitive* mean "untrained," for in many instances such paintings are the work of schooled artists. Indeed, many tribes had highly developed training programs for artists.

About the only way *primitive* could be applied to Indian art is in the sense which includes non-literate societies. But since many of the artists producing this material have certainly proven themselves most literate in public print, even this definition seems inapplicable.

It may seem unnecessary to devote so much attention to this matter, yet it is important to this discussion. Categorizing Indian art as *primitive* has long denied the Indian artist a place in the contemporary white art world. He is forced to exhibit his work, if at all, in shows which are limited in scope, or in specialized museums. He has no opportunity publicly to compete on equal terms with other artists, and he continually finds his work classified as something quaint—interesting perhaps, but hardly art. As a result, he rarely receives stimulation or encouragement sufficient to make him really grow and improve his work to the point where it *can* successfully compete.

At present, of course, he probably cannot so compete—both the mind-set of his audience and his own lack of competitive experience indicate that. But it is impossible to prophesy what might come in time, with suitable encouragement. There is a tremendous waste of latent talent under the present circumstances, and the Indian artist undoubtedly has a great contribution to make, which may some day be realized.

DATING OF INDIAN ART

In order that the reader understands just what is included in anthropological chronology, it is necessary to say a word about the dating of art objects. These can be classified in two main sections—prehistoric and historic.

Prehistoric refers to the period in Indian history which occurred before the written record. For convenience, in most classifications *prehistoric* means "before 1492"—a synonym is *pre-Columbian,* that period before Columbus's arrival. Actually, the meaning of *prehistoric* can vary from one area to another, depending on when white explorers first arrived: precontact times in New England are much earlier than precontact times in Ohio, for example. But for our purposes, any reference to the prehistoric past means sometime before 1492.

The most reliable system thus far developed for dating the ancient past in North America has been the science of *Dendrochronology,* or tree-ring dating, devised by Dr. A. E. Douglass of the University of Arizona. This technique relies upon the fact that trees in the Southwest add growth rings in a rate proportional to rainfall. Counting these growth rings backwards, one can determine how old the tree was when it was cut down. By comparing the width of the rings on different but overlapping samples, it is possible to compute when a given house was built or a certain ruin founded. Overlapping these tree-ring counts enables one to go back into prehistory to 11 A.D. The degree of accuracy obtained from this system is surprisingly high, and is generally accepted by archaeologists throughout the Southwest.

Unfortunately, this system does not work well outside the Southwest. A more recent method is one developed by Dr. Willard Libby, which applies equally throughout the world. Termed *Radiocarbon Dating,* it relies upon the fact that Carbon 14 exists in all organic matter, and is given off at a consistent rate. The rate can be measured and computed against the amount presumed to be present when the given article was "born." By counting backward, a date can be established for the deposit of the article. Some controversy exists concerning the techniques and relative accuracy of this method, but archaeologists are coming to accept it more and more as the delicate measuring devices improve.

Nevertheless, many prehistoric Indian artifacts defeat all such techniques. Some are excavated without adequate records, or data have been lost; the inorganic nature of others defeats C_{14} dating. Unfortunately, this applies to many of the finest objects in museum collections throughout the country. Such guesses are based on experience, comparison with other, similar objects of known ancestry, or on considerable detective work. This may or may not be sufficient to arrive at a close dating— but it is the best we can do. No prehistoric object in North American culture can be dated with absolute accuracy. In most cases the dates ascribed to them in this volume are relative; they represent an attempt to place the article within the period when it is believed to have been made.

For articles made in the historic past, the situation is somewhat better. Documents do exist, and in many instances we have the actual dates when objects were acquired by explorers, traders, or collectors. Many objects can be dated by comparison with similar, known objects. Others are datable by what they are made of, since we know when some materials were introduced—for example, types and sizes of glass beads provide an excellent clue to the approximate manufacture of Plains beaded garments.

For the ethnological articles which are of uncertain dating, we again can only estimate. And these estimates in the historic period attempt to place the object within the century or quarter-century during which it was most probably made.

The earliest object illustrated in this volume would date no earlier than *ca.* 100 B.C. ; the latest was made in 1956. However, most of the specimens were produced between 1800 and 1900 A.D. This period should not necessarily be regarded as the golden age of Indian art. It is simply that most of the objects preserved in museum collections were made during this era. The older— and perhaps finer, who knows?—items have disappeared.

The Antiquarian. Age alone should never be a criterion of art. This is the fallacy upon which the world of antiques has foundered so dismally. There is no axiom with less truth than, "It's good because it's so old." There were just as many, if not more, incompetent craftsmen in the old days as there are today, and we often fall into the foolishness of treasuring a piece of third-rate craftsmanship because it is old, rather than because it is well made or aesthetically pleasing. All too often we ignore the sad fact that the maker's contemporaries would have refused that same piece with disdain.

Some varieties of Indian art have improved in recent times. At no time in his history did the Indian have the facilities with which to produce some of the technically-superb masterpieces like those of the last century. True, often technical fascination overcame good taste, resulting in an overworked *tour de force;* in a few instances improved technique gave rise to improved taste. But wherever there has been careful encouragement and selection, the Indian artist has quickly responded with a high degree of artistry.

The one factor in modern times which has worked against improvement has been economics—the need to produce in quantity, speedily. The pressure to get the job done has removed much of the leisurely approach to perfection which so moved the earlier artist.

THE WHITE MAN AND THE INDIAN

The whole art world of the Indian was completely and irrevocably upset by the appearance of the white man. This strange new person came in several waves, each exerting a different influence. Initially, the explorer brought little and took little; he perhaps levied the least toll.

But hard on his heels came the trader, eager to introduce new things in exchange for local resources. Moreover, what he had to give—cloth, metal, decorative materials—made the greatest single change in Indian art. With metal knives, carving could be done more efficiently; with new cloth, new garment designs were possible; and with the decorative materials such as dyestuffs and glass beads, a whole new world of applied ornament was opened.

Many new decorative materials were used in old ways—this is especially true of beads, which were applied more or less as the older porcupine quills had been. Careful examination of beadwork and quillwork will reveal the debt the one owes the other in style, technique, and execution (Plates 203 and 210).

Next came the missionary, whose whole purpose in life was to influence. By and large, this had a less happy effect on Indian art; there was no sensitivity or interest in native aesthetic abilities, and little tolerance for a differing mode of life. The demand for conformity tended to bring about a loss of freedom of expression in many arts, and Indian religious art in particular suffered at the hand of the incoming nonbelievers.

Mission schools, notably the French convents in Canada, established new design styles, as the young girls were taught to copy European models of the period. This occurred at a time when garment decoration was elaborately florid, which happened to fit in nicely with the curvilinear art so popular with the aboriginal artist. From this set of circumstances evolved an art form still in use today in the Eastern Woodlands region (Plates 244 and 247).

The settler's arrival was of more concern, since it brought a more lasting influence. The household possessions which these newcomers brought with them included many readily usable items which the Indian was quick to adopt. These articles affected art sizes, shapes, forms, and, to some extent, techniques. One example will suffice—the wealthy settler who brought along a few prized Oriental rugs then in vogue started a chain reaction he little suspected. These patterns seem to have made their way into Sioux beadwork (Plate 203), and became popular as "Indian design" when they were taken East with the Buffalo Bill shows. Eventually they turned up in Navajo weaving, after traders gave these patterns out to the weavers, convinced that the beadwork design would make rugs salable in the East.

The whole problem of influence on the artist is difficult to assess in dealing with more recent Indian art. Sometimes it simply defies analysis; one is hesitant to charge that a decorative style was "copied," when it may be only the logical extension of a pattern. At other times, it is a matter of historical record, as at the Santa Fé Indian School (Plates 187 and 190), where a particularly sensitive art department encouraged Indian youngsters to develop an already alive art ability, primarily in watercolor painting. This thrived, and today the so-called "Santa Fé School" presents a definitely recognizable style. As with any "school," it also has limitations and can stifle as readily as it can inspire. Today the work is still active, and individuals of real ability are going far beyond the original scope of the effort.

But, generally speaking, schools and the educational process have not exerted a beneficial influence on Indian art. A vast majority of the schools which include Indian students do not take advantage of their pupils' latent abilities, and often actively tend to train away from them. This has become more marked in recent years. The same attitude is also unfortunately true of most art appreciation courses for white students, which rarely include any degree of consideration of the Indian arts.

The relations of the Federal Government with the Indian in the field of art have a peculiar history. When the Army had the problem of settling the frontier, officers were given the responsibility of bringing back Indian material. This was an early form of the World War II maxim, "Know Your Enemy." It was realized that here was an instance in which the Army was fighting a warrior it knew nothing about; weapons, artifacts, and costuming were collected and studied to learn how best to deal with the problem, identify the wearers, and so on.

Out of this practice grew some fine early collections—many of them contain our best dated examples—but there was little interest or appreciation of aesthetics, as can well be imagined. This was the enemy.

When the Indian Bureau was removed from War Department supervision to that of the Interior Department, the effort remained one of imposing influence on the Indian population. It was not until the late 1800's that there was any tendency toward real interest in Indian culture, and it was so compromised with efforts toward the acculturation of the Indian and the establishment of his way of life along a more European-oriented pattern that it had little effect on art.

In general, Federal efforts attempted to replace Indian ways with white ways. It was felt that this was the best way to "civilize" the Indian. During the period when Commissioners of Indian Affairs were nominated by the church councils, the Government co-operated with the missionary groups in completely halting all expressions of Indian culture—art, language, dance, and custom. The deadening effect this had on Indian morale and psychology needs no comment, and it should not come as a surprise to see how difficult it has been to create any real interest in the Indian to take his place as a vital part of the American community.

Then, in one of the about-faces so historically traditional in all Federal relations with the Indian, a great upsurge came in the middle of the Depression. This was intended to give the Indian a chance to develop his own way of life. It first began in the mid-twenties, under Indian Commissioners Scattergood and Rhodes, but was never formulated by Congress. It was not until 1934, under Commissioner Collier, that the Indian Reorganization Act really put such policies into action. Out of this was the creation by Congress of the Indian Arts and Crafts Board.

Since the work of this organization is not so well known as it should be, it will be of interest briefly to sketch its activities, particularly one achievement which surprised all those who had any connection with the situation.

When the Board was set up, its primary functions were to develop better arts and crafts on the part of the Indian, to promote public interest in these crafts, and to attempt to aid in the production and marketing of these quality manufactures. At the time there was considerable question as to whether there actually was very much "better" quality work available. Fieldworkers were sent to various reservations to discover just what was still being made, since there had never been any serious survey of Indian arts and except for a few superb technical studies made in the early 1900's, most anthropologists were untrained in art as such.

Following this initial survey, it was found that although many craftworkers were still living, few were very active. The severe restrictive measures placed on Indian cultural expressions had successfully discouraged production. By a quirk in the administrative process, it had been thought perfectly all right for Indians to turn out gewgaws and trinkets for curio shops; yet serious art efforts were completely forbidden. Older women, skilled in the arts, had ceased much of their production, and the younger girls had no training or incentive to develop skills.

However, with the encouragement and interest shown by the fieldworkers, together with the removal of restrictive measures, hidden talent emerged. Older women came out of retirement to teach the younger ones, and soon it was discovered that many of the old techniques were not actually gone, as had been feared.

Eventually, as a result of the Board's encouragement, demand for high standards, and assistance at crucial points, a period of peak artcraft production was reached which has continued for about a quarter-century.

In time, as in the past, the governmental attitude again changed, and sympathy with Indian cultural development swung back the other way. While the more recent reaction has never taken the form of the rigid repression of earlier times, lack of sympathy and co-operation has taken its toll. Craft quality declined, arts-and-crafts teaching disappeared from the Indian school curricula, and it remains to be seen whether or not quality production can long support a worth-while market.

Why a Decline? What are the reasons for this tremendous rise and fall in Indian art, other than dictation from above? We have seen that imposition can rarely stamp out a cultural expression completely, and it must be that the culture itself contains some seeds of weakness.

These do exist, and have taken their own toll. The first, I believe, is that the Indian has lost his major market, which was his own people. In the past, a large proportion of Indian art production was for trade or sale to other Indians. This inter-tribal trade is famous in history, but most of it has disappeared today. Thus his creations must of necessity be directed toward a non-Indian market, and he is completely at the mercy of something in which he has no voice or way to control. If that market decides that the fashion one year is to be "Indian," he will find his work in overwhelming demand; but if that decree changes to "Swedish furniture," or "Thai silks," he has no recourse.

Secondly, the pressures of assimilation not only tended to eradicate Indian culture, but also made many Indians refuse to follow tribal arts, which they regarded as a step backward. In their desire to identify with the non-Indian group, they rejected as many Indian characteristics as possible.

Survival by Subsidy? The question may be asked, if an art cannot survive on its own, shouldn't it be allowed to die? Does art, in effect, require a subsidy? Precisely how important is the art of such a small number of people?

It is historically true that any art can and will survive, no matter how it is ignored—providing it is not deliberately and systematically erased. Given the freedom to work, art will make its own way—perhaps not as a prosperous member of society, but certainly as a living, breathing entity. *Prosperity* in art requires encouragement; with apathy, art can only *survive*.

As for the importance of the art of small minorities, it is axiomatic that the art of any segment of society is important to the whole. No group has a monopoly on talent; all can and must contribute co-operatively to the whole, in the proportion that their numbers and talents permit. These contributions must be sought, welcomed, and encouraged. The American Indian's cultural manifestations are one of the few means left by which he can express himself and develop his own self-respect, as well as gain the respect of others. It is interesting to note that not just minimal numbers, but several thousands of Indians support themselves by work in some branch of the arts —thus removing themselves from welfare rolls and, more important, gaining a feeling of independence and personal dignity.

Museums and the Indians. The effect of museums and collections of Indian art on public taste cannot be overlooked. A museum collection is essentially a record of the past, and cannot teach creativity—but these archives of heritage can provide a means of education which may in turn lead to appreciation. Fine collections can instruct the student in what to look for in Indian art, teach the younger Indian something of his heritage, and by displaying superb examples in a dignified, well-installed exhibit, give a prestige which cannot be duplicated in any other way. Carefully selected and well-labeled displays can erase the sense of unfamiliarity with which the average white visitor approaches Indian exhibits, and will introduce him to a fascinating world of color.

Apathy and Indifference. With the tremendous wealth of Indian art and craftwork in the larger museum collections and private

homes, it is perhaps difficult to understand why there has been so little interest in the subject on the part of the general public. This apathy is the more remarkable when one considers the average person's fascination with the Indian of the past.

I suspect that part of the problem lies in some of the barriers to an understanding of the Indian by the white—and *vice versa*. First, there is the language handicap; it is much easier to understand another's culture if one knows how to talk with him. Extremely few white people have any comprehension whatsoever of any Indian tongue. Another handicap is the difficulty in understanding a totally different way of life. Most whites came from, and understand, a European background, with its ideals, values, and concepts; very little of the European way of life shares much in common with Indian cultures.

The factor of mutual hostility and an unfortunate record in dealings with minority problems has also clouded the picture. The Indian early learned that the white man was not to be trusted, and this has not only carried over to the present day, but has also instilled in the white a rather well-developed guilt complex, all of which has built a chasm not easily bridged.

Governmental policies and missionary activities further destroyed possible approaches: a tendency to look down upon other cultures, together with an intolerance for anything non-Christian, was fatal to an appreciation of a differing culture. And governmental vacillations in policy have not helped.

The academic world is, surprisingly enough, not without its share of blame for public ignorance. Many fieldworkers who studied Indians intensively had no art background, and were not art-oriented. Their interest was in tribal origins, linguistic relationships, physical build, techniques of manufacture, and social organization. Art *per se* was not of primary concern, and many of their writings reflect this lack. This is not to accuse, but is simply to emphasize the factors involved in familiarizing non-Indians with the world of Indian art.

In almost every state's school curriculum, the American Indian as a subject is normally taught in the third or fourth grade. The subject is never again considered at any length other than for brief mention in U.S. history classes as part of the westward movement—itself hardly a platform for understanding. Thus the average adult, however well educated and sympathetic, grows to maturity without very much opportunity really to learn very much about, or to understand, this minority group. Very few secondary schools include any serious study of the subject, even in civics or sociology classes. So, unless the individual is particularly interested, or takes college and graduate courses in anthropology, he encounters the Indian again only through the media of television, motion pictures, or the Western story—none of which are noteworthy for edifying portrayals of Indian lifeways.

Since Indians as a group are, by and large, removed from the immediate daily contact of most persons, this indifference can be only too well understood. The Indian is, after all, a very small minority; of the 850,000 estimated population when Columbus arrived, there are today about 550,000 Indians in the United States, and perhaps an additional 50,000 in Canada.

Past and Present. Indian Art, then, has had a tremendously varied history. Long regarded as exotic objects to be brought back from exploring trips or military campaigns, the product of the Indian artist for a limited time supplied frontier people with necessary answers to new environmental problems. Then came a period when the early tourist demands exerted a normal commercializing influence.

Governmental and missionary influences, aimed toward the eradication of Indian customs, slowed any tendency for a resurgence of Indian arts based on newly introduced materials and techniques. The renaissance effected by the Indian Arts and Crafts Board was eventually undermined by another policy reversal. The Indian artist has continually been faced by a bewildering chronology in his relationship with the immigrant to his country.

Today, the primary areas of art production are widely scattered. The largest and most active is the Arizona–New Mexico region, where the Pueblos have maintained perhaps the highest degree of aboriginal art expressions; the neighboring Navajo, Papago, Pima, and Apache groups also retain a strong strain of art activity. Other regions include smaller enclaves in the Plains, the Alaskan Eskimo, the North Carolina Cherokee, the Florida Seminole, and the Canadian Eskimo, as well as tribes in several closely-packed peripheral areas. Yet, with encouragement, all these could expand into healthy art-producing groups, and many of the present knickknack-makers could develop into creative artists. Lacking this encouragement, most of them will eventually disappear.

It would be an inexcusable folly to let this happen, for not only would America lose a great cultural heritage, but no art form is so strong as to be able to afford the loss of such a rich source of inspiration.

LIVING WITH NATURE

Before the White Man Came

Before considering the regional discussion below, it must be emphasized that in no area is there any opportunity for a comprehensive presentation of the true wealth of art possessed by its early inhabitants. In each, there once existed materials and techniques which have not been preserved. We are forced to judge the artistic range of prehistoric Indians by mere remnants—in some instances, a handful of specimens tells us all we know of what was once a widespread art.

We do know that every area was possessed of a lively art sense, for the tantalizing glimpses we get into the past show us a living, vital people, fully aware of the world around them, and making the maximum aesthetic use of their environment.

Some regions surpassed others, of course—due to the materials at hand; the ease of living, which permitted more or less time for artistic pursuits; and perhaps a favorable location, allowing contact with outside tribes which influenced or encouraged artistic expressions.

The tremendous world of color which once existed is almost entirely lost to us; only in the Southwest is there a measurable residue of importance. Yet in every section of the continent, excavation has yielded artwork which still bears traces of paints and dyes, assuring us that decorative use of color was frequent. Many, if not most, of the stone sculptures shown in this volume once bore painted designs; many were apparently covered with paint, and some still bear traces of that coloring (Plates 1 and 41). It is quite probable that in prehistoric times the wooden figurines were also painted.

It is also certain that the early people made great use of grasses, wood, and hides, but these decay rapidly; and, again, it is only in the Southwest that any sizable body of evidence has been preserved. Likewise, other substances must have been utilized in early man's attempt to beautify his world; the many colors nature provided and the substances with which he could decorate himself gave a great canvas upon which to work his talents.

So, bearing in mind that throughout our study of regional prehistoric art expressions we are at best judging only a minuscule portion of the range of techniques, concepts, and materials which must have at one time existed, let us consider what archaeology reveals of the early artist's accomplishments in the various areas of North America.

North by Northwest Coast

It may seem quite unlikely that art would command major attention of the inhabitants of the bleak but beautiful northland. At first glance, there seems little to work with, and the ever-present problem of food supply could be expected to preclude any aesthetic development.

Yet closer inspection reveals many resources for the artist. The waters held ample food, land animals were plentiful, and the long winter nights afforded ample time for doodling. Indeed, it may be said that the Eskimo was the most accomplished doodler in North America; hours were passed in the time-honored practice of working wood, ivory, and stone into imaginative forms. Only a few centuries later, the Yankee farmer would sit around his living-room stove, whittling on a stick of wood, telling stories, and passing the winter nights in much the same way.

Some of the animals the prehistoric Eskimo artist hunted brought treasure with them—particularly the walrus and the whale. Their great ivory teeth and tusks were worked into beautiful carvings, many of which were functional implements, tools, and weapons. The Eskimo even turned the walrus against himself by making harpoon heads and hooks from his tusks.

While much of this carving was utilitarian, a great amount was simply for pleasure, for the northern artist had an eye for the shapely limb of the caribou as well as for the soft contours of the seal. He carved and incised these designs in a variety of ways, experimenting endlessly. In the land of the midnight sun, he had all the time and light he required.

Art styles of this area, insofar as we know them, favor carving in the round, decoration by incising, with presumably some use of inlay. Usually the designs were cut into a bone or ivory base, and then a black pigment was rubbed into the lines for emphasis. Simple linear of circular incising is popular, and a very common motif is the "circle-and-dot," in which many circles are patterned on the surface of the object.

Such wood-carving as may have existed has almost entirely disappeared, but a few ancient burial masks have been recovered in caves, greatly weathered. These have a very strong Oriental cast and have been likened to Chinese and Japanese work. Other than this, little is known of what may well have been a great wealth of wood sculpture.

We know little of prehistoric Eskimo art. In the few excavations of prehistoric sites in Alaska and neighboring Canada, we have recovered only sparse traces of the early inhabitants. We can tell from the scattered evidences that the Eskimo was there in numbers; but there are mostly remnants of dwellings, everyday utensils, refuse piles, and the like, and little of an aesthetic nature.

Several art styles have been classified among those artifacts which do remain, and these emphasize a strongly developed sense of embellishment. Most of the specimens in this category are ceremonial or highly decorated functional implements, but the use of many remains a mystery. The specimen illustrated in Plate 3 is but one of a handful of equally beautifully worked pieces of old ivory, and must stand for the group. It bears the distinctive features of all—a fine sense of proportion, subtle composition, and basic functional form—and conveys the feeling that it was a cherished piece, well worn by years of use. The dot-and-circle motif is still present hundred of years later in similar work from the same region.

Farther south, in Washington, Oregon, and lower British Columbia, there is even less to tell us about the ancient people. It is assumed that in the early days, as now, the major art medium was wood, for apparently the region was heavily forested then, as now. However, no wooden artifacts have survived the effects of a damp climate. Thus we must measure the art ability of the prehistoric Northwest folk by stone carvings and an occasional bone or ivory specimen. A glance at

Plates 4 or 8 immediately indicates their superior quality. These works reveal an art which was certainly not in its beginning stages. They had many centuries of development behind them —and most certainly do not represent a primitive form of sculpture!

It is regrettable that we do not know more about these early Northwestern groups, or of the other ramifications of their art; it must have been spectacular. While some elements persist today in the work of the tribes who are apparently descended from them, the contemporary product seems much less impressive.

The fabulous wood carving of the Northwest Coast artist had presumably not yet made its appearance, unless there were monumental carvings in wood which have not been preserved. Unfortunately, even legends do not help us to know if such carvings existed. The evidence at hand points to a rather sudden flowering of the art, and that in the not-too-distant past.

The Columbia River Basin art world was remarkable in many ways; not only did it reflect a long tradition of sculpture, but its style was also unique in North American Indian art. It is almost as though a group of alien people had suddenly been plopped down in the region. With them, they brought an already well-developed art ability which they immediately proceeded to apply to local materials. These art forms, which were seemingly already of a traditional nature, hint at a great elaboration of function, and thus, by extension, suggest a great wealth of ceremony. The tribes in this area must have remained somewhat isolated. Their work does not seem greatly to have affected their neighbors to the west and north, although a slim relationship is apparent between Plate 5 and Plate 139, in which the use of the "skeletal" motif may have some derived association.

It is not until well into the historical period that we find ample evidence of the richness of art for which the Northwest Coast region proper is so famous today.

Pacific Prehistory

From the Columbia Basin down to the southern California region, the art of the coastal area of the Pacific remains a great unknown quantity. The many early peoples who lived along the coast must have had a rich culture; but little is left of it today, and we must judge largely by what was found when the earliest explorers arrived, together with the work of their descendants. True, there may not have been the wealth of color and sculpture found farther north, but the great technical and aesthetic skills evident in what has survived would indicate otherwise.

In the southern coastal section of California, from the

Channel Islands south to Catalina, we find widespread stone-work, indicating a considerable carving skill. Most of it is made from a local form of steatite. When quarried, this material can be carved rather easily with stone tools; then, like alabaster, it hardens with exposure to the air. With simple tools, a variety of forms was achieved; the whale in Plate 7 would do credit to any carver in naturalistic forms, and it is but one of many similar examples.

A large variety of carved steatite and other stone objects, including mortars, pestles, tubular pipes, charms, and fetishes have been recovered from excavations. Delicately incised shell ornaments are also known, many of which are beautifully inlaid; they were produced in astonishing quantities. Deposits of asphaltum provided an adhesive which was used in extensive inlay work, and an ample supply of brilliantly colored abalone shell, *haliotis,* provided the inlay material. In general, artifacts from this area represent a not inconsequential art ability.

The Southwest: Desert Dwellings and Cliff Homes

Extensive archaeological excavation and scholarly study have taught us more about the prehistoric cultures of the Southwest than about any other in North America. It is only here that we can ascribe specific dates to some cultural activities, establish definite relationships between groups inhabiting the area, and achieve a semblance of cultural relativism of the early peoples.

It is therefore to be expected that here we will be concerned with a greater variety of art expressions. It is perhaps the architecture which distinguishes this region the most. Monumental stone "cliff houses" remain eloquent testament to the superb architectural skill of the prehistoric Southwesterner (*see* page 16). After progressing from a simple pit house through above-ground dwellings to the cliff-dwelling stage, these folks moved out onto the surface of the plateau region in Arizona and New Mexico and built remarkable stone structures. Some were true apartment houses, sheltering hundreds of families in comfortable compartments on several floors. The largest of these, at Pueblo Bonito in New Mexico, had well over four hundred rooms on four floor levels.

While these buildings changed somewhat in time, the concept was never wholly lost, and today the visitor to the Southwest can see the same architectural work in the Pueblo villages of New Mexico and Arizona.

All these structures are of course quaint and picturesque, but they are even more practical, efficient, and well designed for their purpose. The centuries of experience on which their designers could draw have resulted in buildings which surmounted weathering and many environmental problems, and

provided for the social relationships between close family groups and efficient everyday living. Such aesthetic considerations as mass composition and form were not neglected in the process.

The cultures which produced such fine housing facilities also gave us some of our most successful artwork. These people were masters of the applied arts: they were able to take simple forms and decorate them in an amazing variety of designs and styles. Painting was perhaps the most common technique; next came the textile arts, in which basic weavings were frequently embellished with appliquéd designs or embroidery. Most of the ancient Southwestern arts are known by utilitarian articles. The rich ceremonial art which we know existed has largely been lost; some was buried and some deliberately destroyed. Fragile masks, costumes, and ritual paraphernalia either do not exist at all, or else exist only in unidentifiable fragments.

The pottery effigy in Plate 16 illustrates the tendency to embellish utilitarian objects. Whether it was only for ceremonial use or was simply a beautiful *objet d'art*, we do not know; but it shows the Pueblo artist's interest and skill in applied design. This expression was even carried to the extent of weaving intricate designs in color into the soles of fiber sandals—which would not be seen unless the wearer turned up his toes. This sole decoration has later counterparts among the Plains tribes.

Southwestern prehistoric art is essentially lineal; we find little of the realistic painting or decoration which one might expect in such an advanced civilization. Among the known examples of sculpture, only a few are in stone; by and large this was a plastic art, done in pottery. Some stone idols, or fetishes, have been found, but it seems that the artist preferred to do such carving in wood, which has not survived.

The ramifications are interesting. Early pottery and basketry was sparsely decorated; later black-on-white wares became more so, and textile decoration also increased. But it was in the flowering of the Pueblo "Golden Age," about 1050–1300, that really major efforts were exerted toward designing for specific purposes. The great religious arts, in which symbolism and ceremonial figure-portrayal become so prevalent, began to develop, and out of this grew the great cities of the early-historic period, such as Awátovi, Kuaua, Pottery Mound, and others. Recently excavated murals at these sites reveal a hitherto unsuspected wealth of mural paintings depicting the ceremonial life of the period.

The relationship of the prehistoric Southwesterner with his Pueblo descendants shows striking parallels in cultural development. If we interpret correctly, the Pueblo art of today is a closely related continuation of old techniques, affected more by the introduction of new tools than of new ideas.

It should not be assumed that there was only one art form throughout the Southwest. Even in such a relatively compact area as Arizona-New Mexico there were differing concepts and skills. The work of the Hohokám people, as shown in Plates 9 and 10, is marked more by fanciful designs than by the technical skill of people of the more northerly Anasazi area (Plate 16). Though the one is of a different age than the other, there was never the skilled execution and sureness of touch among the Hohokám that was so common in the Anasazi or Mimbres regions.

Nevertheless, the Pueblo area developed a strongly conventionalized art, held to quite rigid forms. There seems none of the imaginative of free-flowing artistic concepts more common farther east. The Southwesterner was more concerned with expressing his art (and his life) in set lines along accepted patterns. In this he also utilized a symbolism that seems unequaled elsewhere, save perhaps among the later Plains folk. But it is fair to comment that the art of symbolism reached its peak in the Southwest.

At its best, Southwestern art is marked by extreme technical competence and fine control of line and form; but it shows little experimentation and rarely ventures beyond set patterns, which are applied and re-applied in many intricate ways. These people were masters of involved concepts, and could play endless variations upon a theme.

The Midwest: Forest People of the Early Days

In this area also, we must pass over many matters concerning aboriginal art expression simply because we lack information. What the prehistoric Midwesterner produced, we can only guess from a limited class of preserved material, together with an attempt to backtrack from present-day descendants.

The great bulk of existing specimens from this section is in stone; some shell has been preserved, and a small amount of metal. Of basketry, textiles, and wood art, only shreds exist—just about enough to assure us that these folk used such material; for the competence, design, and coloring, we have almost nothing to go on. Pottery exists, but it is not of great aesthetic quality, as a rule.

But we must judge, even on this limited basis; and it is certainly fair to say that the Midwestern artist achieved remarkable results with limited tools. He excelled in working stone into the desired forms. Sculpture was well-known, and the stone art of these people was surpassed only by that of their southern neighbors—who may have been distant relatives.

The one natural asset this region offered—metal—was used to the utmost. Copper from the natural mines of the Lakes region—from which came most of the float copper so eagerly sought by the Indians of the Central and Southern United States—was worked into tools, implements, and decorative ornaments (Plates 23, 24 and 30) which are impressive art concepts even today. All the wrought-copper work and the metal incising from this region shows a confidence growing out of long familiarity with the material. This was no recent art, and the designs also show an experience born of long practice.

Much of the stone, shell, and metal art was apparently ceremonial in nature. The function of many pieces is still a matter for heated scientific debate, and assumptions can be dangerous, but in many cases we have little else on which to base our identifications. It is evident that a goodly portion of the recovered specimens had a secular use not understandable in today's terms—they may have been used by people of importance, which would suggest a tremendous economic and social class organization.

These people built mounds and constructed temples on top. They sometimes buried their dead inside the temples, and they erected their homes around them. Some of the mounds were great "effigy mounds," constructed to represent serpents, humans, or animals. These occasionally reached a height of fifty to seventy-five feet, and extended several hundred feet in length. Unfortunately, although they were still being actively used when the first European explorers entered the area in the mid-sixteenth century, very few documents exist to tell us of their function. It is in these several mounds that some of the finest specimens of prehistoric art have been recovered. The Adena, Hopewell, and Tremper Mound areas are among the most exciting sources for early aboriginal art. From one Hopewell site alone, some 145 superbly sculptured stone effigy pipes were excavated (Plate 22)! Many of these had been deliberately broken, presumably as sacrificial offerings at a burial.

These people obviously were not minimal producers. They had artists who could produce quality in quantity. As a result, we have a great wealth of stone sculpture—even though much of it is in fragmentary condition due to earth movement, deliberate sacrificial destruction, or the excavator's shovel. The art is, by and large, a naturalistic expression; there is not the great amount of symbolic, abstract, or non-objective art found in some other areas of North America.

The artists experimented with many materials. Some leadwork exists, mostly as castings from stone molds. Mica, or isinglass, was popular, as seen in Plates 28 and 30; it demonstrates an ability to find inspiration in unusual materials. Fine sculpture was even created out of cannel coal. But stone remained the favorite medium, and it is in various forms of stone that the finest pieces were created.

In the far north, almost nothing exists of this type of work. There has been a limited amount of archaeological exploration in the mid-continent region of Canada, but it has yielded little of great aesthetic merit. No doubt this is because in prehistoric times most of the settling in the region occurred quite late and was apparently never an occupation in force; the low quality of the art reflects a transient population undergoing considerable adjustment to a new environment.

In the Not-so-Sunny South

There is a superabundance of evidence indicating that the Southeast was an area where death lurked everywhere, and that a worship of death was in itself an active practice. The surviving artwork seems to offer full proof of this belief. Throughout the many examples available are suggestions of head trophies, skull sacrifices, and ceremonial regalia which include many indications that there was what has been termed a "Death Cult." Explorers of the region, entering as early as 1540, have left accounts telling of the great attention which was given sacrificial rites, and of the ceremonial pageantry which accompanied them. These descriptions are not unlike the reports of Cortés in Mexico, writing of the Aztecs in 1521.

And so it is that we find warriors carrying trophy heads (Plate 64), pottery vessels in the form of death's heads (Plate 38), and the sacrifice of a victim (Plate 47)—all of which bear witness to death worship. Of further interest is that these three examples, among many others which could be cited, come from Oklahoma, Arkansas, and Tennessee—showing how widespread the practice was.

It should not be thought that this was merely a death-centered culture. It combined simple stone and complex ceremonies. The stone was carved masterfully, and the ceremonies were apparently such as to require finely worked objects for offerings or worship. There was a tremendous variety of these ceremonial objects, many of which had functions not obvious to us today. While many may well have been for secular purposes, they are beautifully worked, and include some of the finest art products ever turned out by prehistoric folk.

In the westerly portion of the South, the great Spiro Mound complex produced such astonishing art creations as the incised shell (Plate 67), which offers rich documentary evidence to the student; the inlaid wood mask with carved antlers (Plate 63), and other objects. Not far away was Moundville, with its great structures, out of which came two of the greatest Indian art masterpieces of the North American continent. The first, a sculptured effigy pipe (Plate 54), is one of the best-known stone pipes to come from prehistoric America; and experts have long speculated as to just what the pose of the figure

indicates. It is one of our best examples of the physical appearance of these early people.

It is the second of these Moundville masterpieces, however, which warrants particular attention (Plate 61). For this carved diorite bowl, bearing the sculptured head of a wood duck, has been nicknamed the "Portland Vase of America", and with reason. The artist who achieved such a notable result with his composition has left us a breath-taking concept—the greatness of simplicity with just enough detail to relieve an otherwise monotonous work. The sleek curve of the duck's neck, the powerful bulk of the stone bowl, and the effect of delicacy (although the bowl weighs over 25 pounds!) combine to impress the viewer with the presence of creative genius.

The Middle South produced many fine incised shell gorgets (Plate 60) as well as stone effigies (Plate 46) for which it is famous. The latter, of which perhaps a dozen are known, were in use when Hernando de Soto explored the area in 1540. In their prime, these stone figures had inlaid shell eyes and were covered with paint; even today they represent a high point in Southeastern sculptural art.

Further to the southeast, in Florida, was an art world little known to most people today. Not only did the aboriginal artist in this region express himself in stone, but he proved his talent even more remarkably by working in clay and wood. The anthropomorphic and zoömorphic vessels (Plates 35 and 45) which were made by these people are remarkable; but it is the wealth of unusual pottery creations which are so impressive. Nowhere in prehistoric North America was there as great a development of form in pottery as was achieved by these people; the sense of balance, interesting variations in form, and the feeling for texture and composition make Florida ceramics an art apart.

These people also had a fine knowledge of working shell and metal, mastered the art of silverplating copper, and even did some goldwork. It is quite possible that this latter metal was recovered from wrecks of Spanish galleons taking loot home from Mexico.

While we have less evidence of artistry in wood than is present in pottery, that which remains presents us with some of the most exciting specimens of wood sculpture in prehistoric North America. In 1894, Frank H. Cushing discovered an area at Key Marco where a quantity of perfectly preserved wood carvings were buried in the mud and muck off the shore. These, when recovered and cleaned, formed a collection of unequaled quality. Many of the wooden pieces split and warped badly upon drying, but a few kept their shape, and demonstrate the tremendous talent possessed by the early Calusa people of Florida (Plates 57, 58, 59, and 62). Some shell was also recovered (Plate 65), but we know little of the Calusa textile arts.

This land of temples, mounds, and monuments was an amazing world. The legends which grew up around it were inflated by the early Spanish and French explorers far beyond reality, so that they came to expect treasures of gold and silver and precious jewels—thus overlooking the real treasure which lay at their feet: a wealth of beauty, color, and pageantry. The frustrating accounts left us by those who first saw these mound folk give only a tantalizing glimpse of what must have been a fabulous extravaganza. The exotic colors, tropical feathers, sculptural and painted works which we know existed must have been a picture to impress even the most bigoted European explorer.

It is difficult to account for the tremendous quantity of finely sculptured stone pipes which are found throughout this region. From the art point of view, some of the finest prehistoric sculpture known may be found among these effigy pipes. In point of quantity, the number which have survived is incredible evidence as to the pipe's importance, and perhaps that of the accompanying ritual of smoking.

The pipes are usually carved from hard stone, and fashioned into forms of birds, animals, humans (Plates 49, 51, and 55 are examples), often so heavy as to make one wonder if they were actually intended for use. Some weigh eight to ten pounds, and are over twenty inches in length; yet these are not freaks, for they are found too frequently and in too many areas. Some may have been used with hollowed-out reeds, which is a common practice with pottery pipes. It may more likely be that many were never intended actually to hold tobacco; frequently elaborate ceremonial bowls were simply used as smoke-blowers. The tobacco is prepared and burned in a separate dish or bowl; the smoker then inhales the smoke separately, and exhales it through the sculptured bowl, which is regarded as a religious object.

Some of the sculptured human effigies created by Southeastern artists are of high aesthetic quality. Some are quite small, and others are larger; but all establish the carver as a person of great talent.

In the graphic arts, it is the incised shellwork that makes the greatest impression. Usually made from the *Busycon perversum,* the hundreds of gorgets which have come down to us depict the richness of the ceremonial life of these people in a multitude of ways. The costuming, complex rites, materials used in ceremonies, and intricate designs are overwhelming. Some articles are so widespread, yet so closely related in design, that it seems likely that they were "membership buttons", worn as insignia by members of particular ceremonial societies. Conceivably these simply represent art styles in common or a popular single design, but it seems much more probable that they had some social or ceremonial connotation. Common designs in this group include the severed head, the coiled snake, the spider, the quartered woodpecker, and the cross.

There is considerable argument on the subject of outside influence on the art of the Southeast, notably from Mexico and Central America. This is not implausible, for too many parallels are apparent. However, while there is a similarity of form and function, I do not think it due to more than occasional trading contacts. It is certain that Indians from these three areas knew each other, and that individuals, and perhaps groups of traders, journeyed back and forth. These would of course leave evidences of their own art styles, which might have been copied or adapted. But the careful student of either area can readily point out an equal number of dissimilarities. If this influence were strong enough to have affected religious, social, or ceremonial systems, it probably would have left a much greater mark on art styles and forms.

A NEW PALETTE

Metal, Glass, and Coal

With the coming of the white man, a whole new world opened up for the Indian artist. Immediately he was able to work in materials which he had not been able to tackle previously. The new metal, iron, enabled him to work stone and wood more efficiently, handle bigger tasks, and achieve results undreamed of in his earlier experiences. To his wife, steel needles meant better sewing, finer seams, and stronger textile work.

The introduction of glass beads not only meant that some older materials might be outmoded, such as porcupine quills, but, more important, it meant the elaboration in decoration of many articles, an expansion of decorative concepts, and the enrichment of many costumes and their ornaments which had not been feasible heretofore. The brilliant colors of the beads caught the artist's eye, and not a few of the resulting color combinations provided a kaleidoscope rather than a blend.

It is interesting that in the early days certain colors were immediately favored in specific areas, or by specific tribes, and others were almost never used. Eventually this tribal individualism began to disappear, and ceased to provide a means of accurate identification.

Perhaps the third most remarkable change in Indian art came with the introduction of coal-tar dyes. The earlier use of vegetable dyes was soon abandoned in favor of the newer commercial colors, which were easier to prepare, of greater effectiveness, and resulted in brighter colors. It is difficult to say which of these factors weighed most with the Indian worker. Later, the near extinction of certain plants became a factor, but this did not immediately affect the arts.

It is certain that the net effect of these three new materials in Indian art produced a color palette and style change which was unlike anything the pre-contact Indian had ever seen. By these three innovations the student can often tell just when certain items were made, and sometimes changes in size, color or texture can even place and date articles which show variations in adapting new materials.

The critic cannot say flatly whether the newly introduced materials and tools had a good or bad effect. It has been neither and both. Many people tend to condemn any Indian-made article which employs aniline dyes, commercial beads, or is cut with steel tools. This is akin, in the white art world, to the condemnation of steel sculpture while praising bronze; or of frowning on casein paintings and accepting only oils. Certainly the results are not the same—nor should they be compared in the same way. In many instances the artist intends his work to be different, and chooses his medium accordingly. Actually, the criterion should never be the medium, but what is achieved. Good beadwork is as valid as good quillwork. Garish colors or sloppy quilling is no worse, and no better, than poorly chosen bead colors, carelessly applied. Each is different, and each can be fine in its own way.

So, with his new palette, the Indian artist made many new things. Some were elaborations of the old, some were copies of the old, and it is these that were often unsuccessful. While he could copy the form, he could not always copy the exact style or achieve the identical results. In trying to do so, he sometimes forced the medium, which is always a fatal error in art.

During the change-over of techniques and media, certain variations did appear. Some resulted from a fascination with new things; some, from a shattering of the Indians' economic base. Not a few came about in the struggle for survival.

Stone sculpture disappeared almost entirely in the historic period. The lack of time for the tedious processes involved, the removal of many tribes from their sources of supply, their inability to transport needed materials, and the shattering of many ceremonial customs—all contributed to this erasure. The introduction of metal containers doomed much of the basketmaker's arts, and the white's inability to understand how to use many Indian articles made them useless as trade items. These were the primary causes for the gradual decline of some arts.

Of course, other arts flourished; the white man proved to be a willing purchaser of certain objects, which enjoyed an increasing popularity. The development of techniques involving new materials and products enabled the Indian artist to achieve surprising successes, along with admitted failures, in the historic period. It is in this light of new artistic growth and technological skills that we shall look at the ethnological work (*i.e.,* since 1492) of the Indian artist.

The Eskimo: Who Created So Much from So Little

Although there were many early explorers in the Eskimo country, particularly Russian groups in the western and south-western part of Alaska, the net effect on the artist was not so immediate as in other regions. For one thing, the Eskimo enjoyed a relative degree of isolation, and only the coastal peoples felt the harsh impact of the outsider and his innovations. Stone and jade tools continued to have important use long after other tribes were fully supplied with those of iron and steel.

Yet the Eskimo did have some metal, mostly from ships or exploring parties, and with this he continued his carving in the tradition of his prehistoric ancestors. The same interest in incised decoration, the use of the dot-and-circle and occasionally of inlay, and the fondness for bone and ivory was maintained. The figurine in Plate 68 is not ancient; yet it could well have originated several hundred years earlier.

One peculiar characteristic of the Eskimo is his interest in natural form. He will look at a stone, a piece of ivory, or other object, until the spirit of that object speaks to him, telling him what is to be carved. He firmly believes that this voice will guide him in the composition, and hence insure artistic success.

Another remarkable quality is the delightful sense of humor to be found in so much Eskimo art. The Eskimo loves a joke, and expresses this in much of his artwork. While comparisons may be unwise, one can perhaps credit the Eskimo with the most expressive sense of humor in art of any of the North American groups. Light touches are found throughout Indian art, of course, varying from tribe to tribe. But I think it is in the

Arctic lands that humor is most consistent. Carvings of humorous scenes and episodes, tricks in wood and ivory, true "funny faces," and a concept of the ludicrous are frequent.

Art styles show a wide variety of form and technique. By and large, Eskimo art is expressed by carving in the round, decoration by incising, and an extensive use of inlay. While painting in color was known, it was very rare, and most pigmentation was achieved by rubbing carbon soot into the incised lines. Where wood is available, particularly drift-wood, it is frequently used for such articles as containers and masks.

The Eskimo is a mechanical genius, in a sense, and much of his carving exhibits an astonishing ability to make "things that work." The fashioning of special tools, the fitting of parts into a whole, and the knack of seeing how to create a mechanical implement is outstanding among these people. During World War II, many military people stationed in the Alaskan area found this ability to be of particular value, and it was not uncommon for an Eskimo helper who had never before seen a particular machine to be able to analyze the function of the equipment and make necessary repairs.

Undoubtedly the most remarkable aspect of Eskimo art, and certainly that which has made it world famous, is the fantastic group of wooden dance masks used in various ceremonies and social affairs (Plates 74, 76, and 79). Many tribes make wooden masks and decorate them with considerable ingenuity. But it is safe to say that no North American aboriginal people have developed the art of imaginative characterization to such an extreme degree. This is surrealism *par excellence*. The combination of realistic, imaginative, and supernatural qualities into one artistic concept is rare, and uniquely Eskimo. The flamboyance with delicate materials and the willingness to add what may seem impractically fragile elements to masks is explained by the fact that many of them are discarded after use; they have only to serve for one performance.

Farther east, Eskimo art is less exciting. Of all the fine work familiar to us today, by far the major portion of better quality art, speaking stylistically and technically, comes from the western Eskimo area. Only in Hudson's Bay and Greenland is there any comparable degree of art interest, and the work there cannot truly rival that of the Alaskan. The Hudson's Bay work is primarily known for its strong monumental creations in steatite. This stone, found in the vicinity, is carved and often colored with lampblack to achieve strong composition. The basis of this art is natural scenes of hunting, hunters, animals, and humans in action. There is a rare display of fantasy or imagination, and an occasional flash of humor. Unfortunately, white influence on this work has been overdone.

It is in the peripheral areas of northwestern Canada and Alaska in which the richest Eskimo art is to be found, characterized by a great individualism and sparkle. It remains strongly naturalistic, perhaps equaled in this respect only by Plains painting and the later water-color work of the Southwest.

Northwest Coast:
The Sculptural Heights of Indian Art

Although there may be too little evidence at hand for such a sweeping evaluation, it seems fair to say that the Northwest Coast best demonstrates the influence of tools upon the artist. For it was the introduction of steel tools which liberated the great talent latent in the Northwest Coast artist, judging by what remains of pre-contact art from this area.

This was unquestionably a great talent. No other area in Indian North America achieved these people's breadth of artistic accomplishment. Other Indian artists possessed equally fine talents in specific fields but no other group produced such a wide range of aesthetically superb objects. The Northwest Coast artists were not specialists; they were masters of all arts save pottery. It was their environment which denied them that one skill. Lush forests provided ample wood for containers, so that they had no need to work in clay; furthermore, no clay resources were available.

Vast cedar forests supplied readily carved bases for the huge totem poles, the small wooden figurines, the masks, and the many other beautiful wooden carvings so beloved of the Northwest Coast Indian. Shredded cedar bark was woven into textiles, clothing, and containers; the bone and ivory of various sea creatures was eagerly sought to be worked into ornaments and implements. A sea creature which provided unique beauty was the lowly abalone, or *haliotis*. Its iridescent shell was prized by all the coastal folk; it was valuable as inlay material and as trade goods, for inland tribes used it for personal adornment.

The social system of the Northwest Coast people did much to develop their art, for theirs was a classic capitalist culture. It was one of the very few aboriginal cultures on the North American continent in which the accumulation of wealth and possessions was the main goal in life. The great man was the wealthy man. To these people, riches were essentially man-made —materialistic properties to be bought, earned, or gained by any of several socially approved methods.

The existence of a purchasing class and a continuing need for impressive possessions developed a supplying class—in this case, the professional artist. The Northwest Coast culture was one of the very few in which Indian art patrons hired talented artists. The artist was "bought," regarded as the patron's property, and commissioned to turn out totem poles, masks, costume paraphernalia, household goods, and so on, in order to establish and advance the sponsor's position in the community.

From today's point of view, this laudable support of the artist had its tragic side: most of the art objects were destined for an unhappy fate. The life-view of many of these tribes was that the greatest thing was to give away all one's possessions. This may seem paradoxical in a culture given over to accumulation of wealth. Yet the logic was simple: the more one gave away, the more one's wealth and prestige improved, for the great man gained position by expressing contempt for worldly goods. Actually, he prized those worldly goods above all else, and wanted back everything that he gave away!

Out of this social system grew the *potlatch,* a murderous game of swap. In this extreme form of megalomania, one chief would hold a feast to which his rival was invited. The host would then give all his possessions to his rival, including the many art objects which his hired artist had been working on. Custom dictated that the rival later return the feast, and give back more than he had received. Failure to do so led to public ridicule; there was no greater disgrace. Thus, inflationary pressures built up, little by little, until family and friends became involved—in extreme cases, whole villages were ruined by the insane drive to give away possessions in the quest for prestige.

To show even greater contempt for one's rival (and, by extension, one's possessions), an individual would not infrequently make a great demonstration of burning his goods. Art objects were often broken up or thrown into the sea. The rival was expected to destroy an even greater amount in return. Thus, many of the treasures in museums today have quite literally been snatched from a bonfire or saved from the sea.

Slaves were killed, families sold into slavery, and tribal groups wiped out in this frenzied game of keeping-ahead-of-Jones. Sometimes a canny operator might carefully throw his possessions into a relatively shallow inlet for later recovery, or rivet his broken "copper" back together for use at a subsequent occasion; but by and large the destruction was permanent, particularly when fragile articles were involved.

Apparently "art appreciation," in the sense we use the term, did not exist in this region. Superb creations were seemingly valued more for elaboration or ostentation than for their aesthetic merit. This is not unique; it is true in our own culture, and is indeed one of the penalties of competition in art.

Nevertheless, while this social organization had tragic consequences for many people, it did develop great artists. In the Northwest Coast area they remain anonymous, as in almost all Indian groups. This is surprising for a region where artists were known and sought after, and certainly regrettable; on the other hand, we do have the names of many of their patrons. Of the artists whose names have been recorded, most have been active within the last century.

The great ceremonial pageants of the Northwest Coast were responsible for some of the most spectacular costumes and masks ever developed by the Indian. The fabulously designed and superbly carved masks, some movable and some static, have no equal in aboriginal art expressions. At their best, they far outstrip anything created in Africa, Oceania, or the Orient, both for artistic design and emotional effect. Many were so large that they were unwearable, and were merely held up in front of the performer; others were completely functional and were carved to fit the head comfortably; a few were even masks-on-masks.

The dancing in which this paraphernalia was used was, by comparison, quite poor. There was none of the precision of the Southwestern Pueblo dancer, nor the intricate patterning of foot movement of the Plains performer. The major emphasis was on visual effect, the appearance of the individual, rather than on what he actually did.

Painting played a remarkably important role in this pageantry. Not only were masks beautifully and carefully carved, but they were also painted in a similarly painstaking manner. In later years, after the introduction of commercial colors, this became an unfortunate addition, for the heavy overpainting frequently obscures the subtle line and shadow of the sculpture.

These people were among the earliest Amerindians to master metal. Apparently much of it was initially obtained from whaling vessels, shipwrecks, and, later, from traders. Copper, iron, and eventually steel were worked in several ways with consummate skill; the Tlingit artists were the leaders in this field. The superb copper mask in Plate 121 reveals a talent for form combined with technical ability which was equaled only in the famous fighting knives of this same tribe (Plate 125).

It is difficult, and perhaps unwise, to try to differentiate the tribal art styles and abilities of the Northwest Coast. Much of it is a matter of personal taste, and even more depends upon individual genius. There has been so much intertribal trading, adoption of individuals into one tribe from another, and enslavement-by-capture of alien individuals that the basic "art styles" have become hopelessly intermixed.

Personally, I think the most obviously exciting and impressive work is that of the Kwakiutl, most particularly in the great movable masks and the powerfully painted *Hámatsa* masks (Plate 97). While in many instances these people so overpainted their artwork as to make it garish, they also used

color to strengthen much of the design. Kwakiutl art is not subtle.

A diagnostic rule for the identification of Kwakiutl art would include those articles which are in general well carved, though rarely delicately so. The designs are powerful, often massive, and are usually clearly outlined. Kwakiutl work is normally painted in strong colors, in which red, green, blue, black, and white predominate. (Plates 91 and 92 are characteristically Kwakiutl.)

The art of the closely related Nootka, Makah and Bella Bella is quite similar, and it is difficult to distinguish from that of the Kwakiutl. These tribes employ much the same colors and carving technique. Several other tribes also use strongly colored tones, such as the Cowichan and others of the Salish tribes; but their carving is much less skillfully executed.

Haida art is marked by precise technical control, and this tribe is one of the few in this region which has exercised its skill in stone (Plates 110 and 113). As emphasized in this argillite work, the Haida carver demonstrates a style with a characteristic form all its own. Haida art is not weak; it may lack some of the Kwakiutl power and impact, but it is fully as expressive. There is less reliance upon color and more upon form and carved detail. Perhaps the Haida may be called the virtuosos of Northwest Coast carvers.

The product of the Tsimshian artist is usually softer, generally more subtle in its sculptural quality, and as the famous mask in Plate 100 demonstrates, includes qualities which place it at the top in creativeness. The Tsimshian was a small tribe, and its work is less familiar, since much of it is frequently confused with that of other tribes.

The work of some tribes, such as the Niska, Kitksan, and Songish, may be less well known because it has been overshadowed by that of their neighbors. However, examples which survive clearly prove their creative abilities were no less remarkable. One of the finest characterizations in existence is the superb mask of an old Niska woman, Plate 93. She is a real person, not a static caricature in wood. The Kitksan rattle in Plate 84 demonstrates a superior technical skill, having been developed subtly from a single slab of wood.

Of all these tribes, it is perhaps the Tlingit which has best found a sound balance between the technical superiority of the Haida and the powerful design and color of the Kwakiutl. Tlingit artists have a complete competence with tools, together with a fine understanding of design, color, and composition. Nevertheless, much of this is expressed with quiet reserve. Tlingit art does not shout at the observer; it relies on quiet understatement; "Here I am—come look at me. Judge for yourself, and you will find hidden richness."

Most of the Tlingit examples in this volume cannot be "seen" at a glance; they require a lingering study. The fine canoe-prow figure in Plate 81, or the delightful small carved ivories in Plates 119 and 120, or the mask in Plate 88—all reveal hidden features when given a second look.

It is unfortunate that the monumental pieces of Northwest Coast art cannot be adequately shown. It seems better to emphasize the same qualities in smaller examples whose proportions illustrate the same beauty and artistic accomplishment than to shrink their eighty-foot length into an eight-inch photograph. Plate 122 shows such a monument-in-miniature.

The stylization of the Northwest Coast artist ranges from extremely realistic to completely abstract. The Eskimo is superior at surrealism, the Southwest artist, at symbolism; but it is the Northwest carver who has done the most, perhaps, with abstract design. His ability not only to abstract the whole animal, but at the same time to see him "from the inside out," and to portray him thus, is beautifully displayed in Plate 129. The subject possesses all its normal features, and they have been abstracted in a manner which results in a variety of related compositions. The artist has simultaneously examined his model as though by X-rays, presenting the vital organs in that manner.

Another Northwest Coast skill is that of fitting designs into given shapes (Plate 103). It would seem that no shape or form was beyond the artist's ability to create a harmonious composition.

Many of this region's designs are of particular interest to Europe-oriented students, for its inhabitants developed an astonishingly rich heraldic art. They employed zoömorphic motifs to designate lineage, position, and heritage in almost the same manner as the English peer of the same period. Just as the latter traced his ancestry through the families of Foxx, Wolfe, Drake, and Steere, so the Indian nobility reckon descent from Raven, Eagle, Owl, and Crane.

These Northwest people lived in great manors, inhabited by many families, each according to his rank. Their homes boasted carved paneling, coats-of-arms, servants, baronial robes, and crowns—the wealthy class lacked no regal splendor. They were the equivalent of a royal family group in the North American Indian social structure, and the art they patronized gave birth to a true golden age.

The California Coast: Poverty in a Golden Cornucopia

The cultural expressions of the tribes along the West Coast, from Oregon to extreme Southern California, were so rapidly eradicated by the early settlers that today we have little of the colorful art which they developed. We do know some-thing of the complex social organization and variety of the tribes involved, and we have a fair idea of the tremendous numbers of languages spoken; but we have only bits and pieces of the various tribal cultures. They were pushed aside by intruders only slightly more advanced than themselves, who preserved little of their way of life.

Perhaps a dozen museums in the world have examples of the artistic wealth which once graced the California area, but none has a full picture. These Refugees from the Gold Rush possessed many unusual and interesting characteristics—from elk antler they made purses, in which to hold shell money (Plate 150), and they used "million-dollar bills" of obsidian, which they ostentatiously displayed at ceremonies, and beautified themselves with local materials in a manner no one else on the northern continent quite duplicated.

Most of these tribes were small, and they lived simply in a richly endowed land. On the surface, their secular life appeared drab, stark, and wretched—but on festive occasions they brought out beautifully decorated baskets woven more finely than those of any other aboriginal people in the world. These tribes employed local bird plumage in techniques equaled only by the ancient Peruvians and the Polynesians (Plate 158).

Nevertheless, all this beauty disappeared with the arrival of the gold-hungry invaders, who saw only the poverty of the brush huts, the lack of clothing, and the apparent low level of culture. That much of this was the result of a mild climate, and also the backwash from an earlier cultural collision with Spanish and Mexican colonists, made no impression on the Forty-niners. The Indian was rapidly shoved into the back country, hunted down and killed, or rounded up and placed on isolated reservations. Under such conditions, art objects soon disappeared, and it is really a miracle that a few individuals still remained who could demonstrate the old arts when interest in them revived during the 1930's. Even so, only the examples of basketry, as in Plate 147, and a limited amount of featherwork, as in Plate 152, were still being practiced by a few workers; from this came a short-lived renaissance in the basketry arts.

Carefully designed basketry was the basic art form; the specific "tribal" patterns utilized were rarely limited to a small unit, but were known to, and often practiced by, several cognate tribes within a given area. One factor was intertribal marriage, as the women took their arts, ideas, and designs to their husband's group. Today it is impossible to distinguish definitely between a basket made by a Hupa or Klamath, or Yurok or Karok, for example.

In this region the advent of the white man proved a misfortune to the Indians themselves and to all connoisseurs of Indian art.

The Southwest: Creators, Copiers, and Traders

It is in this land of sunshine that the richest variety of art expressions is to be found, the most vital artwork still being produced, and the most familiar to the average person. Few artists have been as adept at applying design to various surfaces as the people of the Southwest; it can be said that in the Pueblo penthouse, the applied arts come into their own. The creation of designs which fit into given areas, can be applied onto given surfaces, or can be adapted to specific shapes, is seen at its best in Pueblo art styles.

From prehistoric times to the present the Pueblos have been active traders. We know of ancient travel routes followed by the Pueblo middleman, going from the Pacific Ocean to the hinterland of the Plains, from Taos to the Gulf Coast. And the trader carried merchandise on all these journeys—exchanging turquoise for shells, shells for feathers, and weaving for buckskin. Above all, he absorbed ideas, willingly exchanging concepts as well as materials. These ideas were adapted to local use, discarded if not practical or helpful, or improved upon by local craftsmen.

The newly arrived Athapascans, both Apache and Navajo nomads, often adapted Pueblo work to their own advantage. The Navajo, in particular, learned the textile arts, copied and expanded the already existing sand-painting work of the Pueblos, and later copied silversmithing from Mexican workers. Soon they were masters of arts which they had taken from others, and very quickly they branched out into semi-original expressions, surpassing their teachers, and even putting them out of business in some instances.

The Navajos made some changes, in keeping with their culture. Among the Pueblos, the men weave and the women do the pottery and basketry. However, the Navajos saw to it that the women did the weaving—and they did such a fine job of learning that today almost everyone is familiar with Navajo weaving, but few indeed know of Pueblo textile arts.

This development was largely the result of outside encouragement; the Pueblo weavers had worked primarily for home consumption, plus trade to their neighbors. The Navajos also worked for themselves, but more particularly for trade, and as soon as the white man came, he became a prime goal. Many traders taught the weaver merchandising, and at one point, perhaps three-fourths of the Navajo women were doing at least some weaving for a commercial purpose.

Similarly, silversmithing increased rapidly in importance. Its origins have been traced to a few Navajos who learned the rudiments of metalworking from Mexican ironsmiths in 1853. Brass or copper wire (some from telegraph lines) provided the first raw material, then silver coins; later, traders introduced slug or sheet silver. Atsidi Tsani and Atsidi Chon, the first silversmiths of whom we have record, taught other Navajos, and by 1900 silversmithing had become established as a major art. Today, although some other tribes, particularly the Zuñi and the Hopi, are very productive, the public mind automatically connects silversmithing with the Navajo, and the bulk of silver jewelry sold in the Southwest is made by that tribe.

The Navajo smiths developed some original techniques, particularly in the use of sandstone molds to cast various ornaments (Plate 168). Turquoise was introduced as a set for silver in the 1890's, and few pieces of Indian jewelry today lack this favorite Southwestern gemstone. In contrast to the Navajo preference for powerful silver forms, often massive, with secondary use of turquoise, Zuñi work is delicate, often with hundreds of tiny turquoise settings on a semifiligree base of silver, or with finely-cut inlays of other materials.

Rich mineral and geological resources gave these people color pigments and a sense of vastness which is frequently reflected in their work. This is especially true of Navajo sand paintings. Unfortunately, the dictum that a finished sand painting must be destroyed on the day of the ceremony for which it is made makes exact reproductions impossible. All we have are sketches and paintings of sand paintings, duplications in sand and other reproductions by skilled recorders, and a few photographs. Yet this has become a great art form in which the Navajo are world leaders.

It is somewhat surprising that, with the vast amounts of stone available, these people did almost no sculpture. Theirs is not a worked art; it is greatest when applied. Even the carved pieces found throughout southern Arizona are missing from the more northerly region of the Southwest. There are a few carved stone fetishes, but they have no great aesthetic merit. An occasional clay-modeled work in sculptural form is created, and some pecked or incised petroglyphs complete the general range of Southwestern stone art.

The only marked sculptural trend has been in wood, and this lacks variety. Some of the most powerful work, that of the Zuñi War Gods (Plate 174), is indeed remarkable. These gods have been created for generations, and the form is traditional. The resemblance of the facial form to certain Pacific area carving is notable, as is the obvious similarity to such modern artists as Modigliani. Since these were carved and then set aside to disintegrate eventually, they are rarely seen today, particularly in good condition.

The other, and better known, wooden sculpture form, the Pueblo *Kachina* "doll," has become a favored item for collectors. It is here that the woodworking ability of the artist is most effectively combined with color and feathered elaboration. In earlier times, these were simple stick-form figures with little embellishment; the emphasis was upon the mask, and the body was of secondary importance. As the art became more sophisticated, the body form was strengthened (Plate 175). With the increasing interest of non-Indian collectors and the greater appreciation of the doll's value, the sculpture became more realistic and imitated the form of the dancer (Plate 184). Today some Hopi carvers have achieved extreme realism in their work, and a few have even exceeded the degree of finite detail and costume representation shown in Plate 176.

The actual object which is portrayed in miniature by these figurines includes a beautifully fashioned buckskin or hard leather mask, painted in traditional designs (Plates 180 and 189). These are made by several Pueblo folk, but the Zuñi and particularly the Hopi have developed the art to its maximum. The fine mask in Plate 182 demonstrates how the artist can give his subject an impressive and colorful appearance. These are made of leather; often an old saddle is cut up to serve as a base. It is painted and feathered to provide the identification for the particular *Kachina* to be represented. Of the more than 300 such beings known to the Hopi, there are but few duplications in mask design; thus these people have truly developed an astonishingly wide range in their art form by which to differentiate and identify their supernaturals.

Sculptural qualities are rarely expressed; the *Kachina* is a reflection of the Pueblo preference for the applied arts. The embellishment is almost wholly applied—little of it can be termed sculptural. This is certainly not to derogate the *Kachina* mask, for of all the Amerindian efforts to conceal the human head by various types of painted designs, it remains one of the most artistically successful.

An interesting side aspect of Southwestern art is the degree of specialization which has developed over the years. This was less true in earlier days than at the present. At one time each person was his own provider—both of things for everyday use and for those religious or ceremonial activities in which he engaged. As economic activities in the arts increase, the individual finds it more and more profitable to stick to one article or craft, which he can produce as a single speciality. Thus, the Zuñi and neighboring Pueblo tribes now express their interest in fine detail by specializing in intricate inlay work with coral, shell, turquoise, and jet, while the Navajo turns to heavy casting and strongly designed silver. Heavyweight textiles are usually Navajo, whereas the lighter-weight ceremonial articles, beautifully embroidered kilts and sashes, and finely woven belts are the work of Hopi artists, for the rest of the Río Grande pueblos have almost entirely ceased making these textiles. Basketry is also almost a lost art in the other pueblos, with only the Hopi producing it in any quantity.

Pottery has undergone serious change. While many pueblos still make many clay objects, almost none maintains the great traditions of earlier days. Much of the pottery made today is for the tourist market, and designs and styles have been adapted to suit that demand; surface decoration predominates, and little attention is given to form or to the quality of the pottery.

However, lest this sound like an over-all condemnation of commercialism, it must be added that it is in the Southwest that this influence has been most fully realized. In many instances it may have lessened quality, but in others the discerning artist had the wisdom to maintain high standards and reap the resulting economic benefits. Some individuals were able intelligently to employ new technology to advantage and to cater to the traveler with taste; as a result, their work is well known today and in great demand.

This seems an appropriate place to say a brief word about the future of Indian art, since the Southwest is its most active producing area today. Much of this book concerns the early Classic Period of Indian art. In general this was followed by a decline in quality and aesthetic merit as the impact of acculturation became stronger, traditions were watered down, machine competition became more pronounced, and interest in the Indian declined. This has happened in many, many instances, and, unfortunately, it will continue.

The pressures of today's economic system and the demand for conformity upon our citizens leave little room for the individual differences which are so much a part of the healthy human. The Indian is caught in this, just as the other peoples within the Western framework. As he strives to fit into the pattern, much of his traditional life has to be left behind. All too often, art is part of that tradition.

And the life of the people changes with their economy. At one time, almost every Hopi man wove, every Hopi woman made pottery or basketry; not too long ago, most Navajo men knew silversmithing, and their women were active weavers. Today, less than one out of ten of these artists still practice, and this proportion is declining rapidly.

It is not too late to preserve much of this, but it can be done only by encouragement, understanding, and appreciation. Except for the occasional individual with considerable good taste, a few fine exhibitions devoted to the work of the Indian artist, and a rare instance of nation-wide inclusion of Indian art among the other "American" works, there has been almost no conscious recognition of this art heritage.

44

The Basin and Plateau:
Diggers and Snakes—and Artists, Too

The Basin-Plateau region, which was an early melting pot, has produced some bewildering ethnological problems which are still not fully understood. It was here that so much of the early contact with the white man created problems for both groups. This was one of the few sections wherein the white man was welcomed, Christianity was willingly adopted, and early settlement voluntarily aided by the aboriginal inhabitants. Each of these brought ultimate disaster to the Indian.

Here there were great variations in native culture, ranging from aesthetic heights to unaesthetic lows. A majority of these folk were distantly related to each other—not only by language, but even more importantly, by environment.

Many of the tribes which subsisted on camass roots were called "Diggers" by the early explorers, who looked askance at their mode of life. They were called "Snakes" by Lewis and Clark—a term misunderstood by later travelers and detrimental to Indian-white relations. Both white and Indian had to operate under initially predetermined concepts which made any harmonious adjustment almost impossible.

Actually, some of our better artwork came from this region. The proud Nez Percés and Shoshoni were masters of the painting arts, particularly as applied to hides; the lowly Paiutes wove fine baskets, created clever hunting devices, and supported themselves on a land no one else would have considered livable. Culture, and civilization, is only relative.

Living so close to the Great Plains, these people regularly traveled out onto those vast areas to hunt buffalo; occasional contacts with Plains tribes led to a tremendous cultural interchange, which in turn resulted in a mélange of art motifs. Since the tribes intermarried and moved back and forth through the land, their art cannot always be accurately identified as to origin. An example of this commonality are the flat woven bags commonly called "Nez Percé bags" (Plate 185).

The proximity of the Crow people, whose elaborate beadwork so influenced the horse trappings (Plate 198) of the Plains folk, would obviously greatly influence the Nez Percé, and particularly the Shoshoni. Costumery was radically affected in design and decoration, often with but slight change. Raiding Utes brought back ideas from pueblo, plains, and desert—all of which resulted in an even more remarkably mixed aesthetic expression.

Of these Basin-Plateau tribes, the Paiute is perhaps the least affected by outside art motifs, yet even their culture shows traces of early Pueblo, California desert, and, occasionally, Plains characteristics.

The Great Plains: Artistry in Paint, Bead, and Quill

The Great Plains is the Indian area most familiar to the average white person, for its warriors are represented in the Buffalo Bill shows, Western movies, and TV programs. From this region come the magnificent beadwork art, the buckskin garments, the great feathered war bonnet, and the concept of long fringed shirts. It is the Plains Indian who personifies the race in the minds of most people. And these were colorful people indeed. They include in their large grouping some of the handsomest men, most beautiful women, shortest, fattest, slimmest, homeliest, and the cruelest and kindest people of all tribes. In short, they, too, had a mixed culture.

From the splendid Crow and Blackfoot of the north country through the beautifully dressed Cheyenne and Arapaho to the agricultural Wichita and Caddo, these were at best a fine people, and at worst, a less admirable group. And this is reflected in their art; our finest beadwork comes from this region—and some of our poorest. Plains artists did a limited amount of excellent woodwork—but a larger percentage was less successful. The hide painting of this region is unequaled anywhere—yet some Plains tribes are quite poor at the applied arts.

In short, a member of a Plains group can no more be regarded as *the* Indian than a member of any other similar geographical division. The tribal lines are too fluid, and no one term will encompass all the many types.

Although all these people once had some concept of pottery, basketry, and textile arts, the nomadic life which followed the acquisition of the horse made a radical change in their culture. Some tribes, like the Dakota, came to depend completely upon the buffalo, discarding all pottery which was too fragile for a nomadic existence, and substituting buffalo-hide containers. They utilized buffalo hide in many forms—making bags, pouches, bottles, boxes, and even trunks (Plate 207) from it. This clever form was basically a large envelope, which held an astonishing amount of household goods, food, or clothing.

Everything the Indian made, he decorated. Many everyday articles—used for mundane activities such as poking up the fire, scraping down hides, removing fat, or pounding meat—were beautifully embellished by incising, carving, or painting. This was a leisure-time activity in which both men and women participated.

Art with the Indian had a strong psychological value, as it does with all people. Not all of it had religious or ceremonial content; much was simply to please the user, to make the tool look nicer, or to add a bit of psychological lift to an otherwise onerous task.

Early Plains art was expressed in a variety of ways. Earth

colors on hides, either of deer or buffalo or elk, were worked into incised designs, or painted on with buffalo-bone brushes. Further beautification was achieved by the application of dyed horsehair or porcupine quills. The latter art is uniquely Indian; no other native people in the world developed the use of such material into the remarkable art form which had become second nature to most of the Indians of North America.

The old quill technique was followed, later, after glass beads had been introduced, and the result is often a similar ridged effect, accentuated by Dakota practice of working in repeat-pattern lengths of beads, called "lazy stitching." Occasionally an unwise combination of brilliant glass bead colors gives a poor visual effect. But when good taste is combined with superb craftsmanship, beadwork can express exceptionally fine aesthetic concepts (Plates 203 and 231).

Basketry and pottery were less frequently decorated, and it is probable that the Plains potter never developed a painted pottery to any extent; the prehistoric examples which we now have do not indicate any great amount of painted clay vessels, and the more recent historic work is entirely devoid of applied decoration other than incised work.

In carving, the Plains artist depended almost entirely upon wood. The amount of stone carving was largely limited to stone pipe bowls, mostly made of catlinite (Plate 200). Wood was used more frequently in the eastern Plains, where a variety of objects was made (Plate 221); in the western regions, it was of secondary artistic interest.

The warriors from the Plains ranged far and wide—the Comanche, for example, perhaps traveled farther than any other tribe, going from upper Wyoming deep into Mexico. They knew the people of the Arizona pueblos and those of the Mississippi bayou country. With these wide travels, partially duplicated by many other tribes, came mixed influences on their art and social culture. Some can no longer be traced; others are quite obvious.

The art of the Plains region ranges from wholly realistic and natural to extremely abstract and symbolic. At its best, it ranks with the finest Indian art expressions anywhere. It is unfortunate that the aboriginal culture has been so thoroughly eradicated. Masterpieces such as those in Plates 197, 204, and 211 give eloquent, if tragic, proof of what has been lost.

As in so many cultures, it is the ceremonial phase of Indian culture which inspired some of the most impressive artistic work. One great field of expression was the painted hide shield, which combined many concepts. The narrative type is a fine example of the artist's ability to tell a story in pictures; the symbolism of the shield in Plate 195 was of great importance to its owner, whereas the beauty of design in Plate 213 needed no

more than visual appreciation, regardless of its meaning to the artist who created it.

Much of the artistry of these people was expended upon their person—this we cannot reproduce, alas! The attention given to the Crow coiffure; the face painting, adornment, and make-up of the Cheyenne, and the carriage and bearing of a handsome Dakota man all contributed to this concept of self.

Dancing was vigorous in this region, the kind so familiar to most non-Indians. There was the active "war dance," the lithe body movement and posturing by which war exploits were re-enacted, as well as dances in which more somber and reserved ceremonial rituals were performed, in which body posture was so important.

Not only did the Indian decorate himself and his home, but his possessions and, above all, his horse were ornamented. The fabulous quilled horse-head cover, or "mask," shown in Plate 206 is a magnificent example, as is the gear shown in Plates 198 and 199, which support the contention that no one else in aboriginal North America rode about in such elegance. It must be emphasized that a great deal of this costumery was designed specifically for motion: the artist did not plan his product for static museum display. He had the movement of the body, the graceful motion of the horse, and the wafting of the plains breeze in mind when he developed the corona of feathers, the elaborate fringe, and the many pendants of cloth, leather, and beadwork.

The Midwest:
The Wood and Water Heart of North America

Throughout the great central part of the North American continent there were tribes thoroughly at home in a woodland environment, living around the great bodies of water and developing a distinct culture of their own. They were the birch-bark canoe folk; they made as much from bark as their Plains relatives did from buffalo hide: food, housing, traveling gear, containers, and even clothing.

Their art, then, made great use of the tree; they were master woodworkers, and carving was second nature to them. A fine wood art comes from this area, such as the examples in Plates 220, 221, and 241. The huge burls were lovingly fashioned into bowls for many years' use; limbs and branches were cleverly incorporated into sticks, clubs, or utilitarian implements, and smaller pieces of wood were fashioned into cups, spoons, and tools.

But it was birchbark which had perhaps the most varied use. It was folded, sewn, and worked in many ways and cut, incised, and scraped to produce interesting surface designs (Plate 244). Canoes were made from bark and decorated by several techniques. Small maple-syrup cups were folded into cones and filled with sap, to eventually become "ice-cream cones" of maple sugar. Most of the containers used by the womenfolk were made from bark.

When trade goods were introduced, all this changed radically. For example, the Lakes people eagerly substituted glass beads for the porcupine quills they had worked so masterfully (Plate 231). The new material was used in much the same manner, but there was a greater emphasis on the floral motif, due largely to the European designs learned in convents and from French and English travelers.

In another art expression these people made a remarkably original contribution, by employing silk ribbonwork. The technique apparently was adapted from early piecework costumes of the white settlers. From this the Indian women developed a concept of their own, resulting in something quite new and beautiful (Plate 236). Silk ribbons in both geometrical and floral motifs (Plate 239) were appliquéd to the base material. These costumes are impressive, and their beauty can best be realized when one sees a group with each person wearing a shawl, robe, leggings, dress, and moccasins embellished by brightly colored silk.

Another unique art of the Midwest tribes was yarn weaving, a skill originally perfected with buffalo-hair cording. Many varieties of bags, pouches, and containers were woven (Plate 226), and it is interesting that generally these pouches and bags had different designs on each side (Plates 227 and 228). The same is true of the cornhusk bags of the Plateau (Plates 185 and 186).

In general, the Midwestern tribes made a unique cultural contribution, particularly in their use of wood and costume decoration.

Eastern Woodlands: Planters, Politicians, and Painters

The Eastern Woodlands was the land of the warrior-diplomats of the great League of the Iroquois—the Indians so important during the Revolutionary era.

These agricultural folk used wood, grasses, and bark in their art, almost to the exclusion of everything else. Their harvests of corn yielded husks which were employed in fine braided masks (Plate 230); Indian hemp was gathered for weaving tumplines, straps, and other fiber articles.

It seems unlikely that these people ever did much hide painting. Although they were familiar with elk and deer, there were no great buffalo herds, and no examples of hide painting on the scale common in the Plains area have survived from the Eastern Woodlands. In general, painting does not seem to have been a favored technique, except in the far Northeast.

Basketry was an advanced art, utilizing hemp and cornhusk as well as many varieties of wood, which were made into splints. One innovation from this region was the "rubber-stamped design." Tubers such as the potato were cut into various designs, and these in turn were used to transfer the designs onto the surfaces of the woven basket by means of vegetable dyes. Generally, these designs were geometrical, although floral and linear motifs were also known. Colors were usually pale shades of blue, red, or yellow.

A second art which originated among these folk was the use of shell beads called *wampumpeak,* from which we get the word "wampum." They were strung on thongs and used as an early form of barter-currency, and also ceremonially. The most remarkable wampumwork was in woven belts. The two colors of the quahog shell, white and purple, were combined in a variety of designs to make long belts, bandoliers, or display strips, as well as bracelets and necklaces.

Porcupine quilling was as important an art with these tribes as with the western Indians. In pre-contact times, it was probably the most common and widespread technique of costume decoration. One of the specimens reproduced in this volume (Plate 248) is among the very few elaborately quilled pieces of deerhide which can give us some idea of just how extensive this art was. It may be the oldest datable piece of quilling of such size extant, although smaller examples, such as moccasins, leggings, and so on, are known.

One tribe which developed a specialized porcupine-quill technique was the Micmac of eastern Canada. Although they are not true Woodlands folk, they are discussed here for geographical convenience; together with the Montagnais and Naskapi, they were on the extreme eastern fringe of that culture. Micmac quillwork on bark is deservedly included with Woodlands art (Plate 242).

When colonial traders introduced glass beads into this region, the Indians readily adapted their art forms to this new medium, but they were never so accomplished with glass as the Indians farther to the west. Woodlands beadwork is a pale shade of the great coloration which became the hallmark of the Plains beadworker.

Silverwork was introduced into the region in early colonial times as trade merchandise, and Indian smiths eventually learned the art. It is not generally realized that silversmithing was even more widely practiced in the East than in the Southwest—and at least a century earlier. Today it has almost died out, but many examples of the early Iroquois smiths' work have been preserved.

Certainly the most remarkable and characteristic feature of

the Woodlands folk was their use of the great forest wealth about them. They utilized all the woods in the region; bowls, spoons, ladles, game equipment, and implements were carved from burls, slabs, and branches of trees. Yet the only really outstanding *sculptural* wood carving occurred in the manufacture of the many grotesquely designed False Faces used in Iroquois ceremonies (Plate 233). Many of these were painted to provide greater aesthetic appeal (Plate 235), and some were also decorated with cornhusks, feathers, or buckskin (Plate 234).

One other material which was used only in this region was dyed moose hair. The stiff hairs of the moose were appliquéd onto deerhide. The latter was frequently dyed black to give greater contrast to the softer colors of the vegetable-dyed hairs. Examples of this work are shown in Plates 245 and 247.

Hide painting was most successfully employed by the Naskapi, of the far northeast. The leggings in Plate 144 show the use of the floral "double-curve" motif so frequently seen in the region. At its greatest extent, this painted art was widespread throughout the Northeast and eastern Canadian country. Today it is practiced by only a few scattered individuals.

The Southeast:
Once So Rich—Now So Poor

Upon considering the aboriginal culture of this area, a striking paradox presents itself. First, the population has, in general, undergone a considerable increase; yet at the very same time, the Indian culture has declined in direct proportion. Today, the Cherokee number some 50,000 individuals, and constitute our second largest Indian tribe, yet less is known of their culture than of any other major tribe, and less remains.

The reason is obvious. These people were contacted early in the period of white settlement, and they quickly adapted to white culture. As a matter of fact, their adjustment was so rapid that they lost most of their aboriginal traditions within a few generations. They became so skilled at farming and emulating the newcomer that they were soon serious competitors, and jealousy on the part of the neighboring settlers led to hostility. In 1838-39 came the shameful "Trail of Tears," in which the tribe was forced to abandon its lands and go to Oklahoma, where the people took up a new life amidst many other tribes. This effectively eradicated all but slight remnants of Cherokee traditional culture in Oklahoma. A fragment was maintained by fugitives who hid in the Smoky Mountains, and whose descendants today are represented on Qualla Reservation, in North Carolina.

Little remains of the once-great Muskhogean peoples from Tennessee, Louisiana, Alabama, Georgia, and Florida. The earlier artists of this group were among the greatest in ancient North America.

Only one group, the Florida Seminole, has retained any semblance of its traditions, and they have been tremendously altered by white influences. These people, hidden in remote Everglades areas, have only lately begun to emerge into today's world and take up the new ways—but on their own terms. They have adapted something of this world in their fashions, and an original costumery is well known to travelers and fashion experts as "Seminole" (Plate 224). Of the earlier wood art, almost nothing is practiced today. With encouragement, this could possibly be revived, but it is static at present.

Indeed, of the once-powerful sculptural expressions which we have found all through the Southeast, little remains today except one active group at Qualla. Here, in a co-operative venture organized and encouraged by the Indian Arts and Crafts Board, local Cherokee sculptors have been active in re-establishing the carver's art among their people. Out of this school have come several artists of importance, notably Going Back Chiltoskey, Johnson Catolster, and Amanda Crowe. This is today a thriving enterprise, and the work of the students enjoys wide popularity among art collectors.

But this is essentially due to the strength of the art. Of the related skills, only basketry enjoys a similar vitality. The Cherokees in North Carolina create fine weaves and color combinations, many of which find popular acceptance in white circles. Perhaps the most colorful basketry is that of the Chitimacha (Plate 214). In the mid-1930's these weavers achieved a revival of their art which was in every way as fine as anything done a century before. Their ability to achieve a wide variety of motifs in simple weaves is truly remarkable; yet today almost nothing is being produced by this tribe.

The brilliant beadwork once widespread among the tribes of the Southeast is entirely gone today. The few examples in our museums testify to an original design concept, and several Muskhogean tribes maintained an interesting carry-over from prehistoric art motifs (Plate 205).

Nothing has remained of the tremendously fascinating ceramic skills as exemplified in Plates 34 or 43. The contemporary pottery arts have little to show, and what there is bears little relationship to the fine incised work so superbly represented in Plate 33; the scattered examples of pipe-making, bowl-working, and so on, are a pathetic testimony to the rapidity with which art can decline.

In summation, it might not be unfair to remark that the true "Trail of Tears" is less the trip from the Carolinas to Oklahoma than the Southeastern people's tragic descent from the artistic heights they once enjoyed.

Plates and Commentaries

The following illustrations are a sampling of the varied art expressions of the different Indian peoples of North America, a visual wealth which evolved from a way of life largely gone from our world today. More particularly, it is the product of cultures which made the very most of their varied natural resources. It is abundantly evident that this art developed far beyond the level of mere adequacy, for Indian artists achieved astonishing results in every medium they chose to employ, demonstrating a genuine feeling for form, texture, color and composition. Their work is not merely the product of a limited civilization; it justly deserves comparison with that of other cultures, both of the past and of the present.

It is unfortunate that proponents of Indian art so frequently choose to present the subject in defensive terms, yet it is certainly understandable. There are reasons for this defensive reaction, and many of them have been indicated in the text of this volume. Others are less readily explained. It is a mystery, for example, why our national exhibitions presented in foreign lands have never adequately drawn upon the great wealth of native art—for, of all the American arts, none is so greatly appreciated in foreign lands as is that of the Indian.

While it is certainly unfair to single out anyone in this instance, no one has quite made the point, or revealed much of the reason for this myopic attitude, so well as Catherine Drinker Bowen, in a quotation attributed to her by *The New York Times:* "I have never liked to think about American Indians. I am not proud of the way we have behaved toward them, and I would rather read about something else. John Adams, as I recall, did not like to think about Indians either." If such a point of view can be held by presumably intelligent, well-educated persons, how can one possibly hope to establish a sound democracy? How can one condemn public apathy, if those who would write for that public shirk their responsibility, and remain unwilling to consider on any terms the existence of a minority group? How can the attitude expressed by Mr. Adams a century ago (under quite different circumstances) justify that evasion today?

Perhaps this volume will aid not only in making Americans more familiar with, and proud of their heritage— but will also get people more willing to think about American Indians.

I BEFORE THE WHITE MAN CAME

1

1 Stone Implement

The function of this carefully worked implement is unknown, although there are many unsubstantiated theories. The style is typical of many such stone carvings from the British Columbia region. Traces of red paint suggest that it was once covered with color; it was presumably carried by the loop handle. This specimen was found in a rock cave in Niska Valley by Lt. G. T. Emmons.

Buckley Canyon, British Columbia   L:13½ in.   1200–1600
Museum of the American Indian: 5/5059

2

3

2 *Stone Oil Lamp*

These beautifully sculptured objects, carved from heavy blocks of hard stone, were made to hold a quantity of seal or whale oil. When a moss wick was inserted and lit, they served as lamps in the Eskimo's home. While the incorporation of a human figure into the design is characteristic of this period, the reason for such an effigy is not known; it has been suggested that it represents a spirit. In later times, lamps lost this quality, eventually degenerating into functional but less artistic products.

ESKIMO; Kenai, Alaska   5 × 14 in.   500–1100
University Museum: NA 9251

3 *Adze Handle*

This superb ivory carving has developed a beautiful golden patina from weathering. At one time a jade or slate blade was fastened to the handle with thongs. The butt of this implement ends in a wolf's head; the offset carving of the handle is composed of two walrus heads (only the tusks show in the illustration), which provide a firmer grip.

ESKIMO; Bering Sea Culture, Alaska   L:12½ in.   500–1000
Museum of the American Indian: 2/4318

4 *Stone Club*

Whether used as a ceremonial baton or as a functioning war club, this must have been the prized possession of its owner. The finely detailed carving of the head may be a portrait of some individual, or it may merely be the stylized representation of a man. This is one of the finest examples of stone art from the British Columbia region. The form is similar to other paddle-bladed clubs, common to this region, but their origin and interrelationships are not clear.

Two Mile Creek, Buckley Canyon, British Columbia   L:13 in.   1200–1600
Museum of the American Indian: 12/3273

5 *Stone Mortar*

A variety of animal forms are used as subjects for stone carvings in this area. One such is this quadruped forming the base of a mortar, presumably used in the First Salmon Rite. Although such carvings are characteristic of the whole Columbia Basin and adjoining area, little is known of the culture which produced them. The "ribbed" treatment of the body is reminiscent of the skeletal designs favored by contemporary tribes of this same region, as pictured in Plates 137 and 139.

The Dalles, Wasco County, Oregon   L: 8¼ in.   1200–1600
Museum of the American Indian: 19/337

6 *Petroglyph*

This incised record of a herd of mountain sheep is an example of a decorative stone art form found throughout the western United States. Such designs are often colored in with earth pigments, or painted on flat stone surfaces; these latter rarely survive unless protected, as in a cave. Their use is subject to controversy; many were doubtless simply pictorial representations. Others were probably hunters' tallies or magic wishes for success in the chase. Some are known to have signalized a traveler's passage—a primitive version of "Kilroy was here," so to speak.

Sand Tank Canyon; Inyo County, California   17 × 20 in.   Prehistoric
Museum of the American Indian: 20/3884

7 Stone Whale Effigy

Depicting the killer whale, this is a fine example of the work of the early Pacific Coast artists of Southern California. Although many of these carved effigies have been excavated, their purpose is unknown; it is likely that they were connected with fishing ceremonies. The power of the native artist expressed in such a simple form is a tribute to his ability.

CHUMASH; Catalina Island, California　　　L:6½ in.　1200–1600
Museum of the American Indian: 10/418

8 Stone Mortar

Carved from steatite, this is a characteristic form of the type of vessels found in a limited area of the Pacific Northwest. Little is known of their use or of the people who made them; it is presumed that they served as dishes or mortars. The composition of the seated figure blends in with the foundation animal, and the outstretched arms form the bowl of the vessel. This specimen was found in 1870, assertedly in Washington; it is more likely that it originated in British Columbia, the source of most of these mortars.

Washington (?)　　　　　　　L:7½ in.　1200–1600
Museum of the American Indian: 1/9485

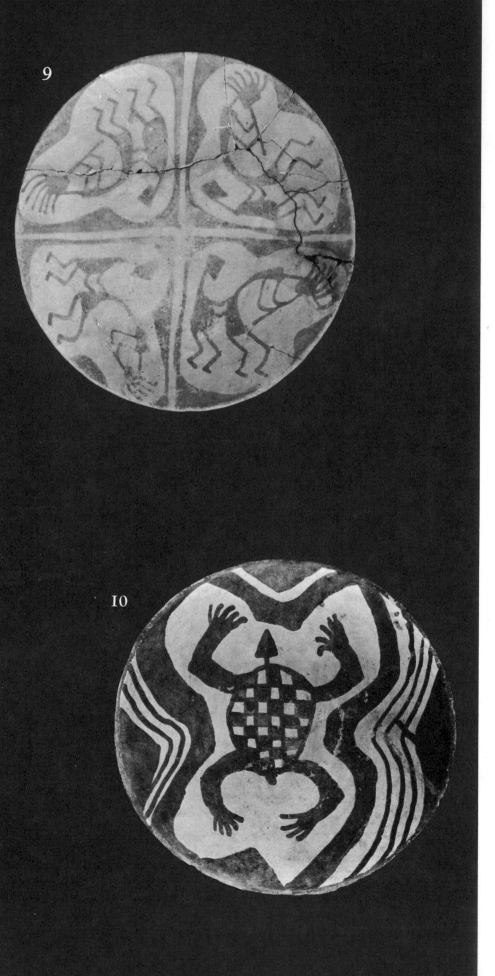

9

10

9 *Polychrome Plate*

An example of ware produced in southern Arizona during the archaeological period termed *Hohokám*. Although the quality of clay is poor and forms are usually not of great aesthetic interest, the designs and motifs used by these people are of exceptional quality. Many of them include delightful, humorous touches.

HOHOKÁM; Snaketown Ruin, Arizona   D:10¼ in. 900–1200
Arizona State Museum: 43855

10 *Red-on-Buff Ware Plate*

Typical of the ceramic art produced by this culture, one of the oldest in the Southwest. The precise identification of the design is impossible to determine; it may represent a turtle, frog, or some similar reptilian figure.

HOHOKÁM; Arizona   D:12 in. 900–1200
Arizona State Museum: 21150

11 *Incised Shell Gorget*

Designs on these ornaments are usually in outline; this is amazingly realistic. It is made from a section of the giant conch, similar to those in Plates 60 and 64. The manner of depicting the animal—a bear or a panther?—seems unique; the treatment of the body almost suggests an X–ray. The eagle is a superb bit of realism. This was found in 1936 by a road construction crew, and is included through the courtesy of Mr. Roger N. Conger.

MOUND CULTURE(?); Oehnaville, Texas   D:5¼ in. 1200–1500
Museum of the American Indian: 22/7574

12 *Kiva Mural Painting*

In 1936 a series of earth-pigment paintings were uncovered during archaeological excavations on Awátovi Mesa. A tremendous range of art styles was discovered, with each layer overlaid on another; as each succeeding painting was made, the old one was simply painted out. The present example apparently shows an underwater scene with fish, frogs, a pike, birds, and other creatures. Above the water are painted bowls containing ears of corn and flower blossoms (squash?). This panel originally extended around three sides of the kiva, and reached to a height of perhaps five or six feet; erosion destroyed some of the top. The restoration is by Watson Smith of the Peabody Awátovi Expedition.

KAWAÍKA-A PUEBLO; Jeddito, Arizona   1600–1650
Peabody Museum

14 *Painted Bowl*

Although the culture which produced this vessel was of brief duration, many critics consider it to have produced some of the finest ceramics in the prehistoric Southwest. Little is known of these people, and students believe that a single artist exerted a tremendous influence upon fellow workers, due to the consistency in technique and style. This scene represents two men covered by a woven blanket.

MIMBRES; Swarts Ruin, New Mexico   D:9 in.   1000–1300
Peabody Museum: 95815

13 *Polychrome Bowl*

This beautifully painted design of a butterfly is representative of a whole class of early Hopi pottery. It was from ware similar to this that the famous potter Nampeyo took the ideas which resulted in a renaissance of Hopi ceramics at the turn of the century.

CLASSIC PUEBLO; Sikyatki, Arizona   D:10 in.   1300–1700
Chicago Natural History Museum: 80942

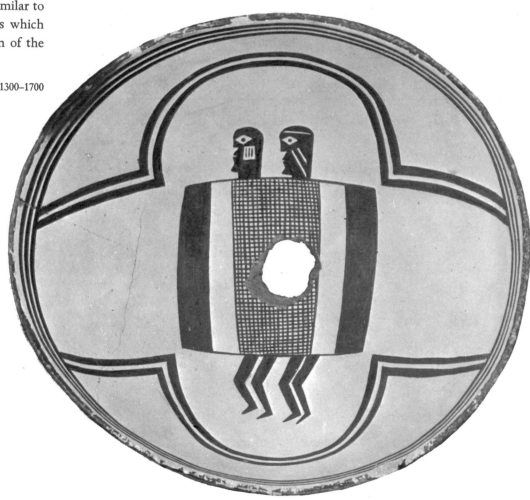

15 *Duck Decoy*

Formed on a tule rush foundation, covered by duck feathers and painted, this realistic hunter's decoy of a canvasback drake is a good example of form in art. Although this is a prehistoric specimen, the same technique is used by modern descendants of these people. The specimen illustrated here is part of a hunter's cache excavated in 1924 by M. R. Harrington.

LOVELOCK CAVE; Churchill County, Nevada   7½ × 11 in.   1000–1400
Museum of the American Indian: 13/4512

16

16 *Effigy Vessel*

Carefully worked clay zoömorphic figures are frequently found in the prehistoric Southwest. Whether these portray animals, incorporate animalistic components in fanciful manner, or are actually made with some fetishistic idea in mind must be left to the imagination. This vessel seemingly portrays some animal, but whether it is an abstraction of a goat, sheep, deer, or other animal, it is nevertheless a striking example of the whimsy of the Anasazi potter.

ANASAZI; Tularosa Cañon, New Mexico   8 × 9 in.   1100–1300
Museum of the American Indian: 18/6406

17 *Flaked Points*

This variety of chipped stone points demonstrates the beauty in form which was mastered by skilled flint workers. Simply as artistic forms, these would attract favorable attention in any art exhibit.

Texas, Florida, and Missouri   L:5 in. max.   Prehistoric
Museum of the American Indian: 2/6027, 22/9, 9/2401, 17/9712

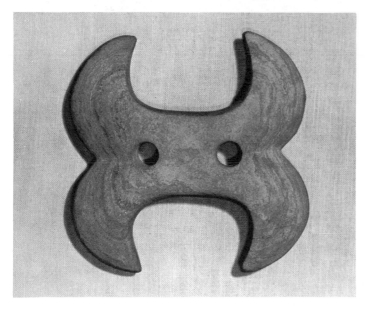

18 *Winged Banner Stone*

The purpose for these implements is not certain; it is assumed that they were intended as adornments or insignia. Many were drilled vertically, perhaps to be carried on wooden staffs; hence the term "banner stones." This specimen, worked from brown slate, is typical of the winged type.

Pope County, Illinois   W:5 in.   1200–1600
Museum of the American Indian: 19/8024

19 *Stone Effigy Head*

Apparently carved and deposited as a burial offering in a mound, this may represent an ancestral figure. It is extremely realistic, and is one of the few masks, or heads, of such type recovered from archaeological excavations. See also Plate 50.

MOUND CULTURE; Heinisch Mound, Ohio   H:6 in.   900–1400
Ohio State Museum: 154/2

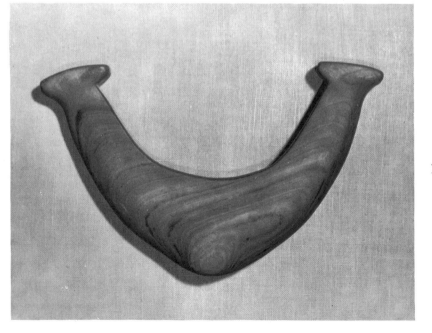

20 *Lunate Banner Stone*

The vertical drilling at the center of this branching implement suggests that it was used on a long wooden shaft, perhaps emblematic of office. Some students also argue that these were used as weights or toggles. This specimen was excavated from a mound near Manchester.

Manchester, Ohio   W:6½ in.   1200–1600
Museum of the American Indian: 4/6801

21 *Pottery Effigy Head*

Whether this is a portrait of the deceased person in whose grave it was found, a deity, or simply an anthropomorphic head, it remains a superb example of early clay modeling. Effigy heads usually are parts of whole figures; isolated and complete examples of this nature are extremely rare.

HOPEWELL; Seip Mound, Ohio   H:3 in.   100 B.C.- 200 A.D.
Ohio State Museum; not catalogued

22 *Effigy Pipe*

This finely sculptured stone pipe, depicting a spoonbill duck holding a fish, is widely known as one of the most artistic of the many Hopewell effigy pipes. The eyes of the bird may at one time have been inlaid, but this is now lost.

HOPEWELL; Ohio   2 × 4 in.   100 B.C.– 200 A.D.
Chicago Natural History Museum: 56750

23 *Bird Ornament*

Apparently this depicts a raven or crow, worked from native copper hammered into thin sheets. The eye is a fresh-water pearl. In prehistoric times pearls were frequently used throughout the Midwestern area and hint at the great wealth of decoration enjoyed by these Indians.

HOPEWELL; Ohio   L:15 in.   100 B.C.– 200 A.D.
Chicago Natural History Museum: 56356

24 *Copper Ornaments*

These cut out pieces were probably sewn on to costumes. They were made from native copper, presumably hammered into sheets, and cut out. If these designs had any symbolic significance, it cannot be analyzed today. It is more likely that they merely had a visual appeal.

HOPEWELL; Ohio   L:6 in. max.   100 B.C.– 200 A.D.
Chicago Natural History Museum: 56188, 56189, 56190, 56191

25 *Sandstone Tablet*

The "Wilmington Tablet," as this is commonly known, is a flat sandstone slab in which a complicated pattern has been deeply incised. Several such stone or wood slabs have been discovered, but their purpose is not understood.

ADENA; Clinton County, Ohio   5 × 6 in.   300–900 B.C.
Ohio State Museum: 3490/210

26 *Fish Ornament*

Perhaps used as a ceremonial costume decoration, this water creature cut from sheet copper apparently represents a species of sucker, or catfish. The purpose for which these copper articles were made is a mystery; about a dozen have been recovered, yet no two are exactly alike. The careful fashioning indicates that considerable importance was attached to the objects, and examination of their workmanship suggests they may all have been made by the same individual.

HOPEWELL; Ohio   L:8 in.   100 B.C.– 200 A.D.
Chicago Natural History Museum: 56177

27 *Ornamental Snake Head*

Most of the copper for these ornaments came from the upper Great Lakes, where the deposits were in almost pure form. It was traded throughout the more southerly regions for various materials. The copper nuggets were hammered into sheets and fashioned into a great variety of forms. This superbly designed snake's head and tongue was cut from copper which had been worked paper thin, then incised with stone tools.

HOPEWELL; Ohio   L:20 in.   100 B.C.– 200 A.D.
Chicago Natural History Museum: 56165

28 *Human Hand of Mica*

This beautifully proportioned ornament is cut from sheet mica. The use of the hand as a decorative motif is very widely distributed throughout the American continent; it is particularly common in cave, costume, and mask art and is also found on other objects. The design is not known to have any common significance among the various regions in which it is employed.

HOPEWELL; Ohio   L:10 in.   100 B.C.– 200 A.D.
Chicago Natural History Museum: 110132

29 *Bone Comb*

These skillfully carved combs were used by women throughout the Eastern Woodlands area, and primarily among the early Iroquois people. This exceptional example made from bone represents two animals facing each other.

IROQUOIS; Monroe County, New York   2 × 3½ in.   1500–1700
Museum of the American Indian: 22/3093

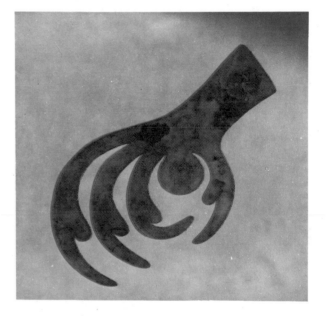

30 *Bird-Claw Ornament*

Made from natural sheet mica, this claw is superbly designed, and the inclusion of anatomical details in such an artistic manner is noteworthy. The function of such a specimen is puzzling, for the fragile nature of the mica precludes any useful application as a costume ornament. It is more likely that these delicate pieces were intended as burial gifts.

HOPEWELL; Ohio   L:11 in.   100 B.C.– 200 A.D.
Chicago Natural History Museum: 110131

31 *Water Vessel*

This vessel is a classic example of Caddoan pottery, long famous as one of the most aesthetically pleasing of its type. The careful modeling and incising show a master hand at work. The scroll design around the central section suggests a close relationship to the later Southeastern beadwork designs, as shown in Plate 205.

CADDOAN; Carden Bottom, Yell County, Arkansas   H:7 in.   1300–1700
Museum of the American Indian: 5/6318

32 *Effigy Vessel*

This clay effigy is remarkable for its realistic qualities as well as for the unusual subject matter. It is impossible to determine whether the person is holding a head or perhaps a mask. Masks from this culture are not unknown, although they are quite rare. Since decapitation of victims was also common practice, the opportunity for speculation is unlimited. Excavated by Joseph Jones from a mound at St. Louis.

MISSISSIPPI CULTURE; Missouri   H:9 in.   1300–1700
Museum of the American Indian: 7386

33 *Water Bottle*

This vessel is remarkable for its fine modeling and incising on a perfectly shaped base, and is among the most beautifully proportioned of its kind. It demonstrates the early Southeastern artist's ability to overcome the lack of a potter's wheel.

CADDOAN; Yell County, Arkansas   H:6½ in.   1300–1700
Museum of the American Indian: 21/5859

34 *Water Jar*

This square-based vessel is well known as a classic example of Caddoan pottery and of the skill and imagination of the prehistoric Southeastern potter. The incised design suggests the scrollwork patterns of later Koasati-Alibamu-Creek peoples. See Plate 205.

CADDOAN: Ouachita Parish, Louisiana   H:5½ in.   1300–1700
Museum of the American Indian: 17/3248

35 *Human Effigy Vessel*

This unusual, sensitively designed clay vessel, partially restored, shows a finely modeled head. It may represent a crouching figure wearing a headdress, and might have been intended to portray an ancestor. Such human effigies are not unknown in Florida, but they are rarely of such fine quality.

Aspaloga, Gadsden County, Florida   H:13 in.   250–750
Museum of the American Indian: 17/3410

36 *Effigy Jar*

This is a fine example of prehistoric Arkansas modeling of the human figure. The designs are painted in a soft red pigment on the cream-colored clay base. What vessels of this type were used for is not known, but their form suggests a relationship to the extensive manufacture of similar vessels in pre-Columbian Mexico.

MISSISSIPPI CULTURE; Yell County, Arkansas   H: 11½ in.   1300–1700
Museum of the American Indian: 20/7434

37 *Effigy Jar*

Of red-and-buff polychrome pottery, this human effigy reflects the great variety in modeling found in the Southeastern area. One of the finest of its type known, this was collected in the 1860's by Dr. E. A. Palmer.

MISSISSIPPI CULTURE; Arkansas Post, Arkansas   H:10½ in.   1300–1700
Smithsonian Institution: 63107

35

36

37

38

39

38 *Head Effigy*

This finely modeled jar representing a death's head may be mute evidence of the practice of taking human trophy heads, supporting a concept suggested in the description accompanying Plate 64. On the other hand, while it may be the head of a slain enemy, it may also be merely that of the person in whose grave this vessel was buried. The whole practice is part of a widespread manifestation throughout the Southeast which archaeologists have termed the "Southern Death Cult." The holes pierced in the ear were once decorated with turquoise or shell beads, as in real life; these have since been lost.

MISSISSIPPI CULTURE; Fortune Mound, Alabama   H:7½ in.   1300–1700
Peabody Museum: 21542

39 *Dog Effigy Vessel*

This vessel demonstrates the realism achieved by the early Tennessee potter. It is also of considerable interest to the scientist, as the curly–tailed animal indicates that the prehistoric inhabitants of the region had domesticated the dog to a considerable degree.

MISSISSIPPI CULTURE; Cumberland River, Tennessee
Peabody Museum: 13998   H:9 in.   1300–1700

40 *Redware Effigy Bowl*

Similar to other feline clay effigies from the Southeast, this delicate vessel has several interesting features. The modeling of the head is extremely well done, and the legs are neatly worked into the over-all pattern. Holes drilled through the vessel walls at the neck and tail ends may mean that there was at one time a cover of clay, since lost. The eyes may have been inlaid, but this cannot now be proven. Excavated at Glendora Place by Clarence B. Moore.

CADDOAN; Ouachita Parish, Louisiana   3 × 6 in.   1300–1700
Museum of the American Indian: 17/3247

41 *Stone Effigy*

Although such finely-carved stone figures are rare in the Southeast, sufficient numbers exist to indicate that there were many of them. Their use is not well understood; some were interred in stone-lined crypts, while others were apparently set up in temples erected on mounds. They may have been idols, ancestral figures, or perhaps memorials to famous individuals of the tribe. Of the two dozen or so known to exist, this is one of the finest in workmanship; even in its damaged condition, it testifies to the hand of a skilled artist. This kneeling woman was doubtless a person of considerable importance in her community.

TUMLIN MOUND; Bartow County, Georgia   H:15½ in.   1200–1600
Museum of the American Indian: 14/1455

42 *Effigy Vessel*

This small pottery effigy jar of a cat or panther shows the characteristic square-headed figurine so popular during the period. Note particularly the scroll pattern and its similarity to the beadwork belt in Plate 205.

Pecan Point, Mississippi County, Arkansas   5 × 8 in.   1200–1600
Museum of the American Indian: 17/3260

43 *Effigy Jar*

Animal effigies are common in the Southeast, but few attain the aesthetic qualities exhibited in this portrayal of a frog. It was recovered intact from a small mound—a rare occurrence with such fragile ware.

Blytheville, Mississippi County, Arkansas   H:7½ in.   1200–1600
Museum of the American Indian: 5/6528

44 *Pottery Bowl*

These bowls are often ornamented with small raised clay decorations. In this instance the design represents a crested wood duck, a favorite art motif of these early potters.

Choctawhatchee Bay, Walton County, Florida   5½ × 13 in.   1300–1500
Museum of the American Indian: 6/230

45 *Effigy Jar*

Presumably an effigy of a pigeon or a dove, this clay vessel is typical of the Weeden Island culture, and belongs to a little-known but remarkably artistic archaeological region. While the ware is perhaps technically of average quality, the imagination and strength displayed by the potters is astonishingly fine; a great variety of zoömorphic forms have been found in the area.

WEEDEN ISLAND; Franklin County, Florida   H:8 in.   250–750
Museum of the American Indian: 17/4088

46 *Human Effigy*

This is perhaps the most famous of the Kneeling Man series, representing the highest degree of the stone carver's artistry. It originated during the period when the Indians erected large earthen mounds to support wooden temples. Early Spanish records report the presence of this type of statue in these temples. Few are preserved today, since many were buried in graves and others were zealously destroyed by white colonists because they were the work of heathens.

TEMPLE MOUND; Wilson County, Tennessee   H:18 in.   1200–1600
University of Tennessee: 1/1 Wil

47 *Warrior Effigy Pipe*

Apparently depicting the beheading of a victim by a warrior, this is one of the most remarkable of the several fine carved stone effigy pipes recovered from the famous Spiro Mound site. The amount of ethnological detail carved into the costume and accessories of the warrior make this a particularly valuable specimen for the scholar, while the artistic concept and powerful composition amply demonstrate the aesthetic ability of the early American artist. This pipe reinforces the many other indications that human sacrifice was common among prehistoric Southeastern peoples.

Spiro Mound; LeFlore County, Oklahoma   5 × 10 in.   1200 -1600
Museum of the American Indian: 21/4088

48 *Human Effigy*

Another Kneeling Man in hard stone, this was one of the earliest statues to have been recovered and preserved in a museum. It is on display at the Shiloh National Military Park Museum, Tennessee.

Pittsburg Landing, Tennessee   H:10 in.   1200–1600
Smithsonian Institution: 271570

49 *Effigy Pipe*

This carving representing a man and a deer is known familiarly as the Lucifer Pipe because of its diabolical leer. A masterpiece of composition, it is carved of red sandstone, and is another of the great works of art recovered from the Spiro Mound in the mid-1930's. This treasure temple of ancient culture was perhaps the greatest single center of the ceremonial life of the Southeastern tribes.

SPIRO MOUND; LeFlore County, Oklahoma H:8 in. 1200–1600
Stovall Museum: B99-2

50 *Human Face of Stone*

The purpose of this carving is unknown; it may have been intended as a mask, as a burial piece, or for display in ceremonies. The partially hollowed-out back also suggests that it served as the face of a wooden statue. It is one of the very few such pieces known from the Southeast. When discovered in 1860 by a Kentucky farmer, there were inlays in the eye sockets; these he pried out with a knife and subsequently lost.

Warsaw, Gallatin County, Kentucky   6 × 10 in.   1000-1500
Museum of the American Indian: 6/397

51 *Bird Effigy Pipe*

Carved from extremely hard stone, this is a most unusual concept. The raised head of the bird gives a balance to the bulk of the body and the heavy bowl, which makes it a superb composition and form. Excavated some time prior to 1875, this was collected by Joseph Jones.

Manchester, Coffey County, Tennessee   L:7¼ in.   250- 750
Museum of the American Indian: 7757

52 *Human Effigy Figure*

Stone figures of this form are found mainly in the Tennessee-Georgia region, and were probably deities or ancestral memorials. Occasional mention of such carved figures by the early Spanish explorers offers ample proof that they existed into historic times. Occasionally male and female effigies are found together. This fine sandstone example was excavated along the Cumberland River in 1885 by Joseph Jones.

Cumberland Valley, Rhea County, Tennessee   H:13½ in.   1300–1700
Museum of the American Indian: 7277

53 *Monolithic Axe*

Such finely carved axes are exceptionally rare, and constitute a monumental tribute to the patience of the prehistoric sculptor working in extremely hard stone. Made from a single block of stone, they are ceremonial replicas of everyday weapons, which had stone heads fastened to wooden shafts. The base is pierced, apparently for attaching a thong or decorative feathers. These implements are found throughout the Southeast and Caribbean region; this one was collected by C. B. Moore at Moundville, and is a companion to those illustrated in Plates 54 and 61.

MOUNDVILLE; Hale County, Alabama   L:12 in.   1300–1600
Museum of the American Indian: 17/891

54 *Squatting Man Pipe*

The significance of the Squatting Man in prehistoric art is difficult to interpret. The subject is known in many examples of their art, as can be seen in Plates 48 and 52. This carved redstone pipe is one of the finest such effigy pipes, and is a tribute to the prehistoric sculptor who produced it. Unlike contemporary practice, tobacco and smoking were not taken lightly by the Indian; they had religious overtones, and elaborate pipes such as this were used for ceremonial smoking only.

MOUNDVILLE; Hale County, Alabama   4×8 in.   1300–1600
Museum of the American Indian: 17/2810

55 Effigy Pipe Bowl

Representing the Horned Owl, this is one of the finest sculptured bird pipes from the Southeast. The majestic bearing of the subject is remarkable, and it would be difficult indeed to improve upon the artist's composition. At one time the eyes of this steatite owl were apparently inlaid, but the material has long since disappeared. Effigy pipes from this region vary tremendously in size; some weigh as much as ten or twelve pounds. Collected by Charles O. Turbyfill in 1926.

East Laporte, Jackson County, North Carolina $4 \times 8\frac{1}{2}$ in.   1200–1600
Museum of the American Indian: 15/1085

56 Ceremonial Maces

Fashioned from stone by flaking, these were deposited in mounds as offerings or sacrifices. Traces of paint on this pair indicate that they were originally painted red and white. They probably duplicate an original wooden weapon, and their form is similar to that shown in Plate 64. Such weapons are of extreme interest because of their similarity to implements found in pre-Columbian Mexico.

SPIRO MOUND; LeFlore County, Oklahoma   L:14 in. max.   1200–1600
Museum of the American Indian: 18/9334, 18/9335

57 Turtle-Head Effigy

Carved from soft wood, this is one of the several effigy sculptures excavated at Key Marco by Frank H. Cushing. Most of them immediately warped and shrank, but this is among the few which retained most of their pre-Columbian character.

KEY DWELLERS; Key Marco, Florida   L:4 in.   1000–1600
University Museum: 40715

56

57

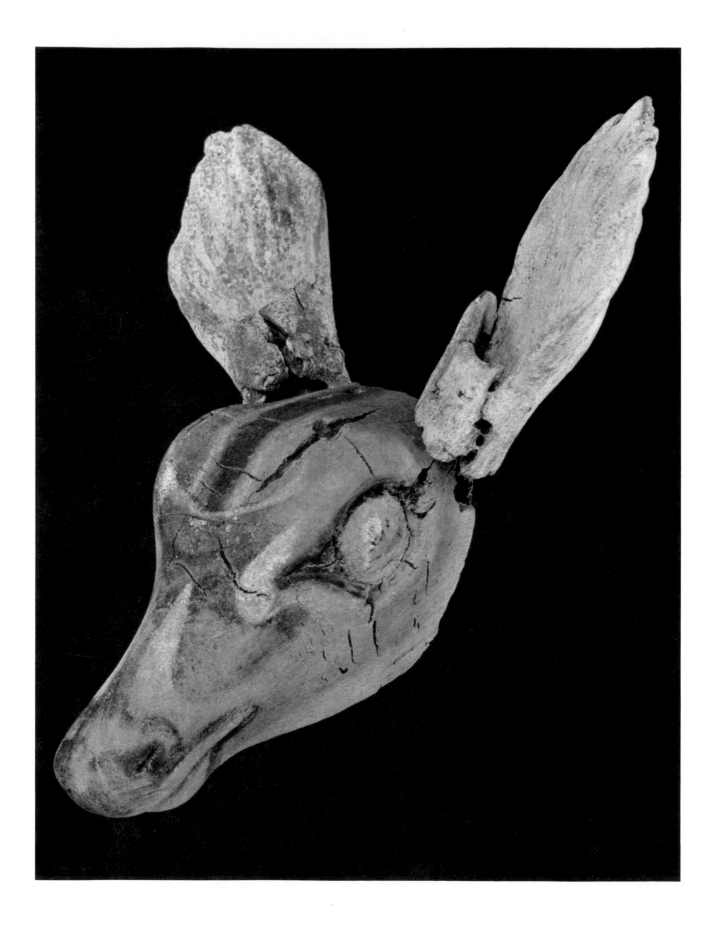

58 Deer-Head Effigy

This is perhaps the finest single piece of carving found at the Key Marco site. It has a sensitivity in concept rare in pre-Columbian art, with an exceptional degree of realism. The use of these various effigies can only be guessed; probably they were not only ceremonial, but fulfilled a mimic-magic role. The surprising amount of paint still visible gives dramatic evidence of the beauty originally presented by this masterpiece of sculpture.

KEY DWELLERS; Key Marco, Florida   5¼ × 7¼ in.   1000–1600
University Museum: 40707

59 Wooden Bird's Head

Another of the fine carvings excavated by Frank H. Cushing in 1895, this graceful head of an albatross shows the unusual force and aesthetic taste of the Key Dweller people. Whether all these effigy heads were produced by a single hand is not known, but their similarity is so striking as to suggest such a possibility.

KEY DWELLERS; Key Marco, Florida   4½ × 3 in.   1000–1600
University Museum: 41240

60 *Shell Gorget*

The human figure is costumed in the elaborate dress of the early Mississippi people. The S-curved design emanating from the mouth is believed to symbolize speech. This, the ornate headdress which suggests the modern-day roach, and the stylized limbs, are features which are consistently found on this type of ornament.

MISSISSIPPI CULTURE; Mississippi   D:7 in.   1300–1700
Chicago Natural History Museum: 68554

61 *Crested Wood Duck Bowl*

Unquestionably one of the greatest examples of prehistoric North American Indian art in existence, this bowl, carved from a single block of diorite, stands alone in simplicity and grace. It is a tribute to the technical skill and patience of its creator, and emphasizes the remarkable ability of early artists to create beauty from simple forms. Excavated in 1905 near Mound R by Clarence B. Moore.

MOUNDVILLE; Hale County, Alabama   10 × 12 in.   1300–1600
Museum of the American Indian: 16/5232

62 *Cat Effigy*

This carving of a seated cat or panther is a companion piece to the other fine sculpture discovered by Frank H. Cushing. The resemblance to the famous Egyptian figures of the god Bast is remarkable, and it is interesting to note that two completely disparate cultures discovered the same qualities in their feline models, and utilized a parallel composition.

KEY DWELLERS; Key Marco, Florida   H:6 in.   1000–1600
Smithsonian Institution: 240915

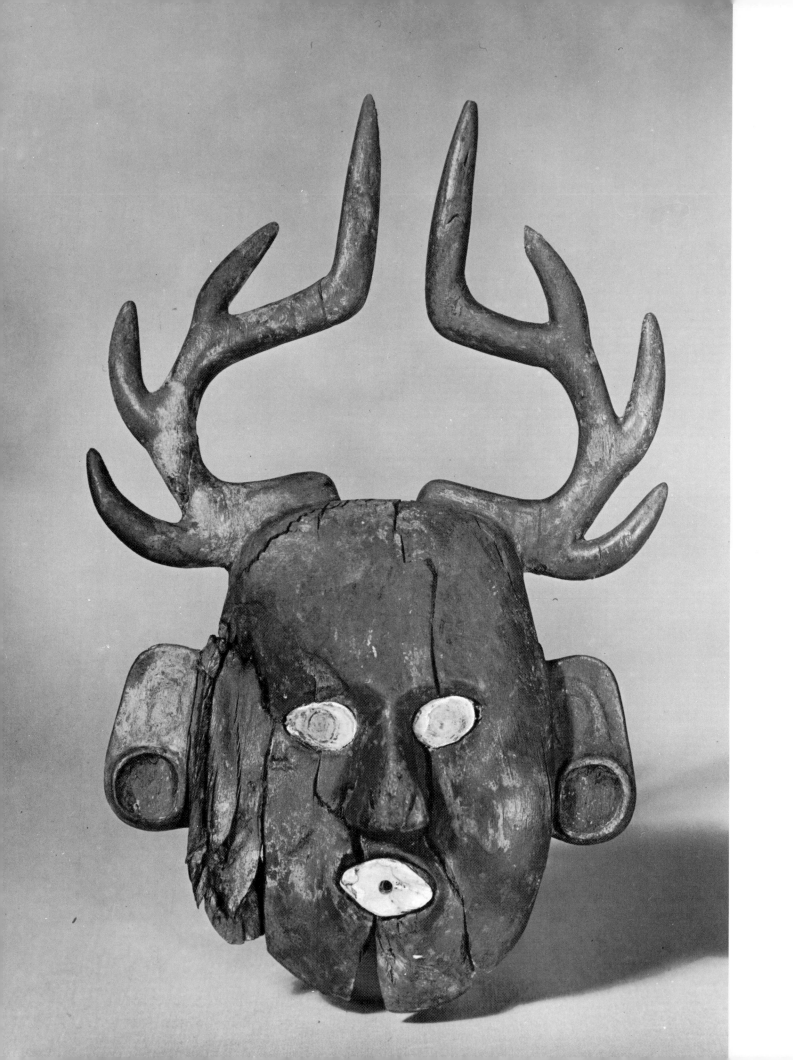

63 *Wooden Mask*

This one-piece carving is among the very few prehistoric wooden masks which have been recovered from the Southeast Woodlands people. It has warped slightly, but the carver's skill remains clearly apparent. The original painted surface on the face has disappeared, and the two shell inlays in the ear lobes are lost. This mask was probably worn during the Deer Ceremony, which we know existed among these tribes. The finest mask of its type known, it is tantalizing evidence of the quality of wood sculpture familiar to the Spiro people.

SPIRO MOUND; LeFlore County, Oklahoma   7 × 11½ in.   1200–1600
Museum of the American Indian: 18/9306

64 *Shell Gorget*

One of the most famous examples of shell art in North American archaeology, this specimen gives a fascinating variety of prehistoric culture traits. The scene depicts a warrior apparently dancing with the head of his victim—eloquent proof that head-taking was practiced. Several articles which have been recovered by archaeologists are pictured in his costume, and the mace held in his hand is undoubtedly of the type illustrated in Plate 56. This piece has long been of great interest to those studying Mexican influence in the pre-Columbian Southeast. It was found in a mound at Castalian Springs, together with three equally well carved smaller shell gorgets.

Sumner County, Tennessee   D:4 in.   1200–1600
Museum of the American Indian: 15/853

65 *Painted Human Figure*

This little man painted on the valve of a sun shell may represent a dancer in costume. It is one of the few paintings on shell, not incised, which have been recovered from pre-Columbian sites; usually the pigment is entirely lost in excavated specimens of this nature. The outline sketch technique is remarkably like contemporary cartooning.

KEY DWELLERS; Key Marco, Florida   L:3¼ in.   1000–1600
University Museum: 40796

66 *Shell Gorget*

One of the most unusual of the many fine carved shell ornaments from the Southeastern region, this incised gorget was cut from the side of a large conch shell, *Busycon perversum,* and has been drilled for suspension on the breast. The characteristic head, eye, and facial features should be compared with the other art objects from the prehistoric Southeast, notably Plates 41 and 64.

SPIRO MOUND; LeFlore County, Oklahoma   D:4¼ in.   1200–1600
Museum of the American Indian: 18/9084

67 Incised Conch Shell

One of a series of conch shells from the Spiro Mound, this Eagle Man is important for its aesthetic qualities and for the great wealth of ethnological information contained in the costuming. Many of the artifacts shown on this shell have been recovered from archaeological excavations, and this shows how they were used. Presumably portraying a ceremonial dancer, this is thought to represent part of an elaborate Spiro ritual.

SPIRO MOUND; LeFlore County, Oklahoma   L:13 in.   1200–1600
Museum of the American Indian: 18/9121

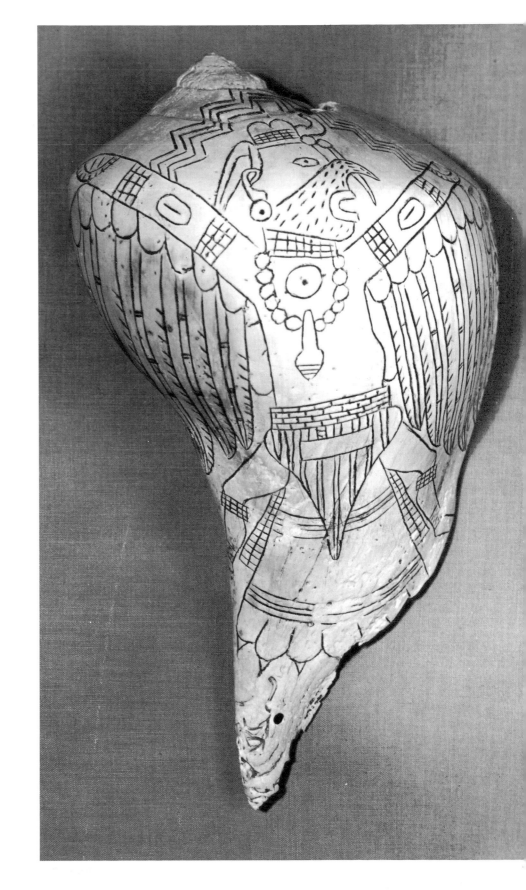

II THE HISTORIC PERIOD

68 *Shaman's Figurine*

This small ivory doll is a fine example of the charms used by shamans in ceremonies. The two circular inserts on the face are inlaid blue trade beads, representing the labrets customarily worn by these people in the old days.

ESKIMO; Banks Island, Northwest Territories   H:5 in.   1800–1850
Museum of the American Indian: 5/9838

69 *Drum Handle*

Carved from walrus ivory, this is a fine old specimen of a utilitarian implement with highly decorative qualities. The holes are for rawhide lashings; the drum rim fits into the square-cut notch. Handles of this sort are used with the large flat single-faced round drum.

ESKIMO; Point Barrow, Alaska   L:5½ in.   1875–1900
Museum of the American Indian: 21/804

70 *Man's Pipe*

A characteristic form, copied from early Russian pipes, this is carved from walrus ivory with black pigment rubbed into the incised designs. Similar pipes were made from wood and inlaid with lead or ivory. They were intended for sale rather than for regular use. The bowl is carved of bone.

ESKIMO; Little Diomede Island, Alaska   L:14 in.   1850–1900
Museum of the American Indian: 6/8649

68

69

70

71 *Shaman's Doll*

This superb example of ivory carving has inlaid copper eyes. At one time it was dressed in a costume, which has long since been lost. These figurines were used by shamans in ceremonies, and are made of a variety of materials. Apparently this one's ears and nose were ornamented with beadwork which has since disappeared.

ESKIMO; Point Barrow, Alaska   H: 9½ in.   1850–1875
Museum of the American Indian: 7/7096

72 Wooden Mask

This carving emphatically demonstrates the strong influence of Eskimo art upon neighboring peoples—in this instance, on an Athapascan Indian group living adjacent to the Kuskokwim peoples. This mask, used in the *Gy-Yema* feast, represents one of the Up River People, who are regarded somewhat as country bumpkins by the more sophisticated inhabitants along the lower courses of the river. Collected by Lt. G. T. Emmons in 1916.

INGALIK; Anvik, Alaska   H:22½ in.   1900–1916
Museum of the American Indian: 5/8667

73 Wooden Mask

One of the finest carvings of its type, this brooding Spirit Mask has tremendous emotional power. Were its origin uncertain, it would seem that the sculptor was portraying a baboon, and that the specimen originated in Africa. Yet comparison with other Eskimo masks reveals many examples related to this particular concept.

ESKIMO; Kuskokwim River, Alaska   H:11 in.   1875–1900
Cranbrook Institute of Science: 3225

73

74

74 Wooden Dance Mask

Carved from driftwood, fantastically designed masks such as this are used in various feast ceremonies, and reflect an intensely individualistic art concept. The mask represents *Walaunuk,* meaning "Bubbles, as they rise up through the water." Such magnificent pieces are too large and fragile actually to be worn; rather, they are held in front of the performer to identify his characterization and actions.

KUSKWOGMIUT ESKIMO; Kuskokwim River, Alaska   L:20 in.   1875–1900
Museum of the American Indian: 9/3432

75 *Wooden Mask*

This complex design apparently depicts a wolf holding a seal in his mouth. The hands and feet presumably represent a spirit. Although this composition is simple and the carving powerful, the idea behind the mask is extremely involved.

ESKIMO; Good News Bay, Alaska   L:11 in.   1875–1900
Museum of the American Indian: 12/907

76 *Wooden Dance Mask*

Used in a similar fashion to the mask illustrated in Plate 74, this specimen represents *Negakfok,* the Cold Weather Spirit, who likes cold weather and storms. He looks sad because he hates the approach of spring, when he must leave the people. Such masks are usually burned after use.

KUSKWOGMIUT ESKIMO; Kuskokwim River, Alaska H:30 in. 1875–1900
Museum of the American Indian: 9/3430

77 Wooden Seal Mask

A simple design, depicting the *inua* of the seal. Comparison of this simple carving with the more elaborate masks in Plates 73, 74 and 76 demonstrates the tremendous range of complexity in masking art produced by this group. Collected in 1885 by J. H. Turner.

KUSKWOGMIUT ESKIMO; Kuskokwim River, Alaska   H:9 in.   1875–1900
Museum of the American Indian: 2/446

78 Parka and Boots

Made from caribou fur, carefully trimmed and decorated, garments of this design have become familiar to travelers in the Arctic regions because of the practical defense they offer against the winter weather. Although indeed bulky, the design and attractive decoration of the clothing keeps it from looking cumbersome or ungainly. The art is still active today.

ESKIMO; Bering Straits, Alaska   L:Parka, 58 in.   1900
Brooklyn Art Museum: 36.42, 36.32

79 Wooden Mask

This unusual mask illustrates the Eskimo belief that all creatures have a spirit, or *inua,* which can appear at will. Made from driftwood and painted in soft colors, it represents the seal and its *inua* in an imaginative manner.

ESKIMO; Good News Bay, Alaska   L:12½ in.   1875–1910
Museum of the American Indian: 12/910

80 *Effigy Statuette*

This carved cedarwood mother and child is included to indicate the bewildering variety of art forms found in Northwest Coast art. When compared with other examples of such carving in this volume, the disparity is immediately evident. The most likely explanation is that this represents a small group of sculptures created by artists who were part Haida, part Hawaiian, and who expressed both art forms in their work. Such marriages were not uncommon in the early whaling days.

HAIDA; Queen Charlotte Is., British Columbia   H: 23 in.   1800–1850
Primitive Art Museum: 56.335

81 *Male Effigy*

This exceptional carving of cedarwood was intended for use on the prow of a canoe. The flowing lines of the kneeling man remove any stiff or static feeling. The representation is that of the Land Otter Man, a powerful being who figures prominently in Tlingit mythology. The head has human hair set into the crown line, the eyes and eardrops are of abalone shell and the teeth are of opercula.

TLINGIT; Chilkoot, Alaska   14 × 21 in.   1825–1875
Museum of the American Indian: 1/6713

82 *Wooden Rattle*

This so-called "chief's rattle" is carved from two pieces of cedarwood, sewn together with cedar fiber. The design is common to several Northwest Coast tribes, and usually consistently portrays a raven with a human reclining on his back. The man holds a frog's tongue in his mouth, in the act of sucking out a poison which was believed to be helpful to shamans in working spells. The frog's body emerges from a hawk; the rounded underside of the raven's body is carved to represent the sparrow hawk.

HAIDA; Skidegate, Queen Charlotte Is., British Columbia L: 13 in. 1850–1875
Museum of the American Indian: 1/8028

83 *Effigy Figure*

This cedarwood carving of a white woman displays to advantage
the skillful portrait ability of the Haida artist. This woman may
have been a teacher, or the wife of a missionary, settler, or
seaman. Such figurines were frequently made as gifts or me-
mentos, or they were made to be sold to travelers.

HAIDA; Alaska   H:8 in.   1825–1875
Cranbrook Institute of Science: 3221

84 *Shaman's Rattle*

Although aesthetically superior to most, this is typical of the
round rattles of the Northwest Coast tribes. The design represents the beaver; the hatched area is his tail. This specimen
shows the careful work which went into the manufacture of
such articles. The rattle is made of two hemispheres of cedar,
bound together and fastened with metal pins. The opposite
side is equally well carved.

KITKSAN; Skeena River, British Columbia   L:11½ in.   1825–1875
Museum of the American Indian: 9/7998

85 Wooden Mask

This mask was collected by **Lt. G. T. Emmons** in 1919 from a deserted grave house at Tuxikan. The animals carved on the cheeks and over the eyebrows represent mice, and recall a legend of the Mouse Man.

TLINGIT; Cape Prince of Wales, Alaska $7 \times 10\frac{1}{2}$ in. 1900
Museum of the American Indian: 9/8036

86 Bear Mask

This wooden mask is an excellent example of old Tlingit carving. The eyes are inlaid with abalone shell, while the teeth are opercula from the red top-shell. Contrary to popular belief, real teeth were rarely used on these masks. This represents the spirit of the Brown Bear, and has small brown bears carved over the eyes.

TLINGIT; Klukwan, Alaska $7 \times 11\frac{1}{2}$ in. 1800–1850
Museum of the American Indian: 9/8030

87 Spirit Mask

This unusually elaborate mask, carved from cedarwood, emphasizes the extreme wealth of design occasionally incorporated into such ceremonial pieces. The mask represents a spirit with a frog emerging from his mouth. Over the forehead is a land otter, while three frogs are carved on the side of the spirit's face. This was collected in 1919 from the Auk shaman by Lt. G. T. Emmons.

TLINGIT; Point Lena, Alaska H:13 in. 1825–1875
Museum of the American Indian: 9/8032

88 *Wooden Spirit Mask*

This very elaborately carved mask represents the spirit of an old woman with a frog emerging from her mouth, reminiscent of an old legend. On either cheek is the otter, while land spirits decorate the band across the forehead; other otters and frogs are on either side of the band. The eyes are inlaid with old Russian trade buttons, and the eyebrows are made from sheet copper. Collected from an old Hoonah shaman at Gaudekan by Lt. G. T. Emmons.

TLINGIT; Chichagof Island, Alaska   H: 13 in.   1825-1875
Museum of the American Indian: 9/7989

89 *Bear-Paw Rattle*

This smoothly finished two-piece yellow cedar rattle, representing a face peering out from a bear's paw, is an excellent example of a motif occasionally seen in Tlingit carving. This rattle formerly belonged to Chief Shakes, a famed leader in the northern Alaska region.

TLINGIT; Wrangell Island, Alaska   5½ × 11¼ in.   1850-1900
Washington State Museum: 955

90 *Wooden Dance Mask*

This is not only a fine example of mask carving, but is of interest in demonstrating how one tribe often took over the designs and ceremonial ideas of another. This mask represents *Xoáexoae*, the Earthquake Dancer, who is believed to shake the earth when he performs. He is depicted accompanied by four spirits and a guardian bird, and is the Kwakiutl adaptation of the Cowichan being whose mask is shown in Plate 135.

KWAKIUTL; Vancouver, British Columbia   H:20 in.   1875–1900
Museum of the American Indian: 6/9153

91 *Movable Mask (closed)*

Another fine example of the changing-face mask; in this illustration it is closed to show the outer face. By pulling the strings, an inner mask is revealed. The mask represents a man's head surrounded by two mythical fish.

KWAKIUTL; Vancouver, British Columbia   16 × 24 in.   1850–1900
Museum of the American Indian: 14/9626

92 *Wooden Mask*

A representation of the Octopus Spirit is indicated by the prominent eyes, hooked beak, and "suckers." This is not a movable mask, but simply a regular mask worn or carried by shamans in ceremonies. The stylization of the octopus by merely suggesting the tentacles is a fine example of Northwest Coast symbolic art.

KWAKIUTL; Cape Mudge, British Columbia   20 × 22 in.   1875–1900
Museum of the American Indian: 11/5216

93 *Wooden Mask*

Representing an old woman wearing a labret, this is the finest known example of character portraiture from the Niska tribe. It is rare to find such startling realism in Northwest Coast art, and this classic piece shows how the native artist can meet such a challenge. The labret, inlaid with abalone shell, is a common form of facial decoration among these people, but such an ornate one would have been worn only by the wealthiest of women.

NISKA; Upper Nass River, British Columbia   7 × 9½ in.   1825–1850
Museum of the American Indian: 9/8044

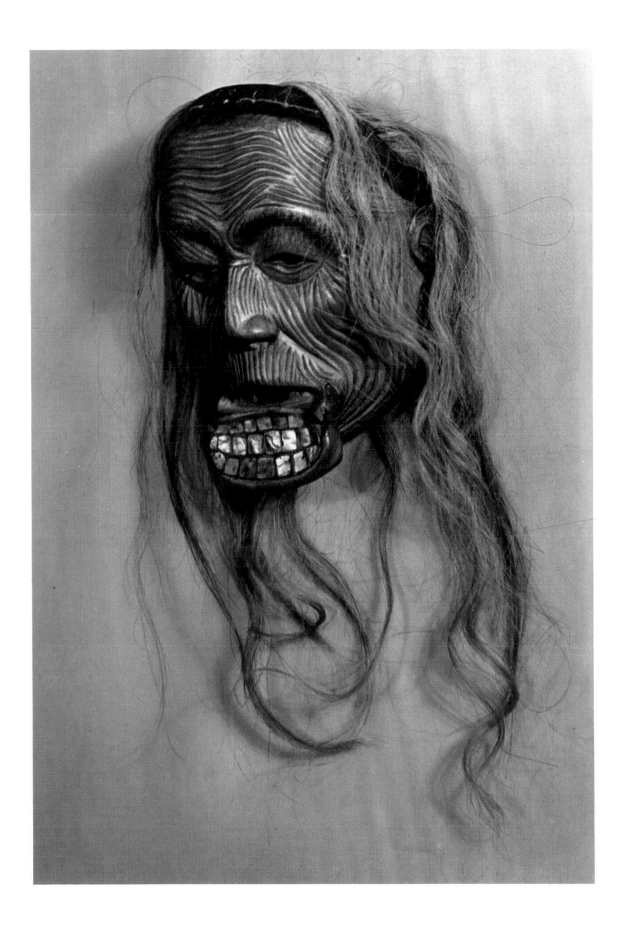

94 *Movable Mask (open)*

Masks like this were worn by shamans in various ceremonies. During the dance, strings were pulled to open out the covering mask, revealing an inner carving. Some masks of this type were so constructed as to present three or four different representations. This movable feature of mask carving was most highly developed among the Kwakiutl, although it was also known to other Northwest Coast people.

KWAKIUTL; Cape Mudge, British Columbia   H:21½ in.   1850–1875
Museum of the American Indian: 19/8963

95 *Wooden Mask*

This mask depicts a poor woman, wearing a simple labret. The artist's ability to use the grain of the wood to best purpose, and to finish his work with great care, is outstanding in this fine specimen. Compare the labret worn by this woman with the more elaborate ornament of the wealthy woman illustrated in Plate 93. This was collected in 1907 by Lt. G. T. Emmons in the Nass River country.

NISKA; Kitlakdamik, British Columbia   H:10½ in.   1850–1900
Museum of the American Indian: 1/4234

96 *Shaman's Mask*

This mask represents a cannibal spirit who lives in the mountains. One mask shows the spirit, whistling to attract the passer-by; the other, his dead victim. The Janus-head concept is occasionally found throughout the Northwest Coast area, and this is an unusually fine example of wooden sculpture.

NISKA; Aiyansh, Nass River, British Columbia   H:10 in.   1850–1900
Museum of the American Indian: 1/4238

97 *Wooden Mask*

Depicting a wolf with the skull of his human victim, this is similar to the well-known Raven Masks of the Northwest Coast region, and like them is used in *Hámatsa* ceremonies. The collar is shredded cedar bark, so sewn on as to help conceal the wearer.

KWAKIUTL; Vancouver, British Columbia   18 × 18 in.   1880–1900
Museum of the American Indian: 21/6535

98 *Fish-Killing Club*

Carved from red cedarwood, this represents the sea lion. These clubs were used to kill halibut or other fish when they were brought into the boat. The designs varied with the imagination of the carver, but usually the owner's clan or some magic representation of the fishing arts was included. The eyes are inlaid with abalone shell.

TLINGIT; Klukwan, Alaska   L:20 in.   1855
Museum of the American Indian: 5/6897

99 *Carved Elk Antler*

Probably used as a slave killer, this implement once had a blade inserted in the slot to provide an effective cutting point. Such elaborate weapons were occasionally employed at *potlatch* celebrations when slaves were killed by a blow on the skull. Since slaves were highly valued, this gesture served to demonstrate the wealth of the feast-giver.

HAIDA; Queen Charlotte Is., British Columbia   L:15 in.   1825–1857
University Museum: NA 3360

100 *Wooden Mask*

This is one of the best known, and quite possibly the finest, Northwest Coast mask in existence. It possesses a quality of sophisticated carving and quiet beauty achieved by very few sculptures among the American Indian peoples. It was collected early in the nineteenth century and taken to England by an unknown explorer. The fringe is of human hair.

TSIMSHIAN; Skeena River, British Columbia   7 × 9½ in.   1800
Museum of the American Indian: 3/4678

101 *Box Drum*

Carved from red cedarwood, with totemic designs, this type of drum is not known elsewhere in North America. The two animals carved on the front of this drum represent the bear and the frog, apparently the owner's clan.

TLINGIT; Alaska   H:35½ in.   1850–1875
University Museum: NA 6828

102 *Wooden Club*

More elaborate than most, this fish-killing club bears designs representing the eagle, killer whale, a man, and a bear. It is not a particularly old specimen, and was most likely carved for sale, but it is a fine example of the modern technical skill of the Northwest Coast carver.

HAIDA; Queen Charlotte Is., British Columbia   L:29½ in.   1900
Museum of the American Indian: 6/9458

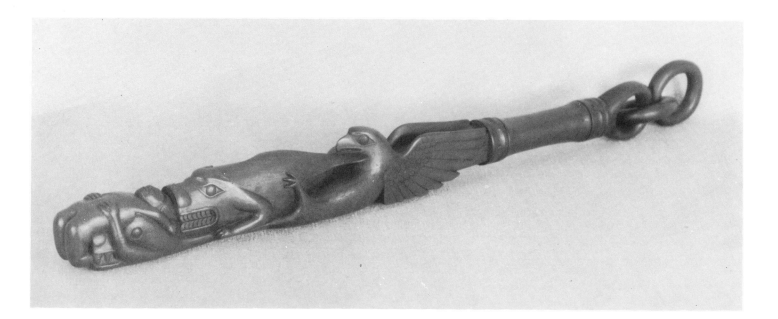

103 *House Post*

Such beautifully carved cedar posts were erected in the interior of the great Northwest Coast houses, and indicated the importance, family ancestry, and social position of the owner. This specimen is one of a set of four; designs on the remaining there are similar but not identical to those on this post. A careful analysis will reveal the head, body and limbs of an animal carved in the style so characteristic of the region.

TLINGIT; Klųkwan, Alaska   H: 91 in.   1850–1885
University Museum: 31-29-13

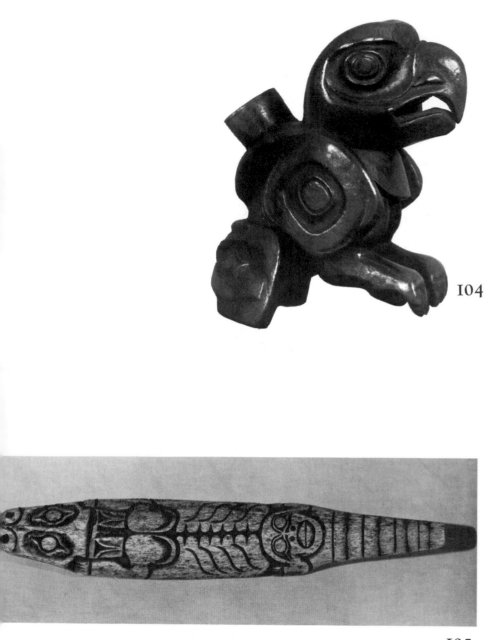

104

105

106

104 *Pipe Bowl*

This pipe bowl was carved from cedarwood, and depicts an eagle, presumably the totem or clan of the owner, the Gonaho chief at Dry Bay. A metal tube, usually of brass or copper, is worked into the design, and holds the tobacco. The stem is simply a reed or stick with the pith removed; it is often thrown away after use.

TLINGIT; Alsek River, Alaska   H:3 in.   1850–1875
Museum of the American Indian: 9247

105 *Bone Club*

Carved from whalebone, the design on this club shows a flattened-out representation of a sea creature, possibly a sea otter. The head, limbs, vertebrae, and body of the animal are clearly seen.

KWAKIUTL; Vancouver, British Columbia   L:12½ in.   1850–1900
Museum of the American Indian: 21/125

106 *Pipe Bowl*

The Northwest Coast practice of incorporating legends into art motifs is interestingly demonstrated by this fine cedarwood pipe. It portrays the legend of a woman who was stolen by a mountain. The two wolf heads at the base represent the guardian spirits (foothills) of the mountain. The human head is of the captive woman, and the column itself is the mountain. The hawk and sea lion heads represent family totems. This pipe was collected from Chief Shakes of the Stikine people.

TLINGIT; Wrangell Island, Alaska   H:8½ in.   1850–1875
Museum of the American Indian: 1/2927

107 *Wooden Comb*

Carved from red cedar and inlaid with abalone shell, this comb portrays a raven curved over his prey in an off-center design style so popular with the Northwest Coast artist.

TLINGIT; Alaska   2½ × 5½ in.   1860–1890
University Museum: NA 4265

108 *Argillite Carving*

Commonly referred to as "slate carving," this kind of work is
done only by the Haida. The stone comes from a quarry near
Skidegate, Queen Charlotte Islands. It is soft when worked, and
hardens following exposure to the air. This scene shows a boat
filled with oarsmen; the white inlays are of bone.

HAIDA; Queen Charlotte Is., British Columbia   6½ × 12½ in.   1850–1900
Museum of the American Indian: 13/1875

109 *Ornamental Carving*

Made of maple wood, this fine example of technical skill
represents the best combinations of talent, tool, and material.
The design represents a man caught by a giant clam, and
drowned as the tide came up.

TLINGIT; Alaska   4 × 16 in.   1880–1900
Washington State Museum: 2288

110 *Argillite Carving*

This carving represents an episode in the legend of the Bear Mother. In it, the berry picker is giving birth to her bear child; two grizzly bears are assisting her. This remarkable composition is one of the extremely few Amerindian works portraying Caesarean section. It was reputedly carved by the versatile Charles Edensaw, the famous sculptor.

HAIDA; Queen Charlotte Is., British Columbia   7 × 7 in.   1875–1900
Museum of the American Indian: 19/3521

111 *Pipe Bowl*

This pipe is carved from argillite, commonly called slate, which is found only on the Queen Charlotte Islands. The composition demonstrates one variety of the more involved art styles of the Northwest Coast. The symbolism in such complicated designs is often fully understood only by the sculptor or his client. Such pipes were made primarily for trade purposes, and were rarely intended for smoking. The present specimen was collected by Gov. William Clark, and given by him to George Catlin, the artist, sometime before 1832.

HAIDA; Skidegate, Queen Charlotte Is., British Columbia   L: 13½ in. 1800–1832
Museum of the American Indian: 1/9272

112 *Ceremonial Hat*

These elaborately carved and painted hats were worn by wealthy men on formal occasions. The decorations indicated the family affiliations, importance, and wealth of the owner. This wooden hat, named "The Noble Killer," belonged to the chief of one of the most powerful Tlingit clans. The design bears the effigy of the killer whale, indicated by the fin upright on the crown. The inlay is of abalone shell, and the locks are of human hair.

TLINGIT; Klukwan, Alaska   H:10½ in.   1850–1875
University Museum: NA 11741

113 *Argillite Carving*

This is the famous "Bear Mother" carving by Tsagay. It is probably the best known single piece of carved argillite from the Haida, and one of the few of which the artist's name is known. The figures tell the legend of Skoaoga, who married the Bear chief; their child had a human form but bear instincts. The sensitivity and emotion shown in this piece is remarkable, and the plastic quality of the composition is rarely seen in Indian art.

HAIDA; Skidegate, Queen Charlotte Is., British Columbia   L:5¼ in.   1883
Smithsonian Institution: 73117

114 *Chief's Hat*

Woven from cedar bark and painted with raven designs symbolizing the clan of the owner, this fine hat is typical of the basketry headgear worn by important Northwest Coast men. The blue cylinders on the crown indicate the number of *potlatch* celebrations held by the wearer; the streamers are of weasel fur. Four such feasts had been given by the owner of this hat, who was the equivalent of a millionaire. Such affairs often resulted in financial ruin, since strict rules of prestige demanded that a man must outdo his rival in giving away his possessions.

TLINGIT; Sitka, Alaska   H: 14 in.   1850–1875
Museum of the American Indian: 17/6251

115 *Argillite Carving*

Representing a sculptor with his hammer and chisel, made of carved ivory. The man is dressed in a kilt similar to that illustrated in Plate 129.

HAIDA; Skidegate, Queen Charlotte Is., British Columbia H: 9¼ in. 1875–1900
Museum of the American Indian: 13/8311

116 *Feast Spoon*

Carved from cedarwood and inlaid with abalone shell, spoons like this were used at *potlatch* celebrations or for other village feast occasions. This specimen demonstrates the considerable skill of the artist in incorporating his designs into the shape of the article. Many of these spoons were three or four feet long.

TLINGIT; Wrangell Island, Alaska   L: 23½ in. 1850–1900
Museum of the American Indian: 2/6103

117 *Ivory Shaman's Charm*

The dorsal fin indicates this is a representation of the killer whale; it is carved from moose antler and inlaid with abalone shell. Such charms were fastened to the costume of the shaman, and used as symbolic fetishes.

KITKSAN; Kitwanga, British Columbia   L:6¼ in.   1850
Museum of the American Indian: 9/7954

118 *Ivory "Soul Catcher"*

Shamans used such carvings to capture persons' souls in ceremonies. It was believed that when such an implement "swallowed" the person's soul, he became the shaman's prisoner. The design, ornately inlaid with abalone shell, represents *Sisiutl*, the mythical double-headed water monster.

KITKSAN; Kitwankul, British Columbia   L:8 in.   1850
Museum of the American Indian: 9/7935

119 *Shaman's Charms*

Carved from antler, such charms were used to decorate a shaman's costume. They represented a variety of spirits which he called upon to aid him in his ceremonies. The one larger piece depicts a spirit canoe made in the shape of a sea lion and an octopus; in it are seven spirits. The smaller charm combines a sea creature and the Double-Headed Monster.

TLINGIT; Sitka and Wrangell, Alaska   L:5 in. max.   1825–1875
Museum of the American Indian: 9/7948, 2/2089

120 *Shaman's Charms*

These three charms were carved from walrus ivory, and show the great variety of designs used for costume decorations by Northwest Coast shamans. The largest, from Hoonah, represents the Raven; the central carving is a Wolf's Head from Angoon. The smallest specimen was collected at Sitka, and combines a Spirit, a Crane, and a Bear in its design.

TLINGIT; Alaska   L:5 in. max.   1825–1875
Museum of the American Indian: 4/1669, 11/1816, 1/2154

119

120

121 *Mosquito Mask*

Copper masks from the Northwest Coast are extremely rare, and this one, representing the Mosquito, is among the fines, examples known. Most metal masks are rather crudely workedt but this specimen is remarkable for the sensitively conceived design and the skillful handling of the sheet copper. The eyes and mouth are inlaid with abalone shell. This mask was collected from the Chilkat people by B. A. Whalen before 1905.

TLINGIT; Klukwan, Alaska   8½ × 14 in.   1825–1850
Museum of the American Indian: 6981

122 *Effigy Pipe Bowl*

Carved from walrus ivory and inlaid with abalone shell, this representation of a squatting man is a superb example of the exquisite carving sometimes found in Northwest Coast pipe bowls. This is an unusually powerful composition for such a small work, and was collected among the Chilkat by Lt. G. T. Emmons.

TLINGIT; Klukwan, Alaska   H:2½ in.   1825–1850
Museum of the American Indian: 9204

123 Copper Shield

Fabricated from sheet copper and incised with totemic designs, these were important objects of social and economic prestige. Not only did they indicate the wealth of the owner, but they also served as money in the sense of a security. "Coppers," as they were commonly termed, were frequently given away at *potlatch* feasts to show the extreme wealth of the owner; occasionally, in a supreme gesture of contempt, they were thrown into the sea. The rival plutocrat was then expected to remove the insult by outdoing his competitor and giving away two. Canny exhibitionists sometimes broke the copper into pieces, then later riveted the parts together.

TLINGIT (?); Alaska   H:30 in.   1800–1850
Brooklyn Art Museum: 05.260

123

124 Copper Rattle

The incised design on this rattle represents a bear, perhaps an ancestral figure of its owner. The eyes are inlaid abalone shell. The form is typical of the region, and is created of two hemispheres of hammered copper mounted on a wooden handle and bound together with leather. These metal rattles were used only by very wealthy or important individuals.

TLINGIT; Alaska   H:9½ in.   1825–1850
Southwest Museum: 980-9-131

125 Fighting Knives

The Tlingit were among the first Indians to make use of steel, which they obtained from shipwrecks. The typical fighting knife demonstrates their ability to work this and other metals. The specimen with a carved wooden head, which depicts a Chilkat chief, is inlaid with abalone shell—as is the superb ivory-handled weapon. One of the finest examples of their steelwork, the longest knife once belonged to the chief of the Hutsnuwu people.

TLINGIT; Angoon, Alaska   L:21 in. max.   1825–1850
Museum of the American Indian: 8/1841, 1/2504, 2/8702

124

126 *Dance Kilt*

Of trade cloth with dentalium shells sewn on to form the design, this kilt is similar to the apron in Plate 127, and is used for the same purpose. The designs represent a bear shown in X-ray fashion: the face forms the body, with another face above it, and the spread-out limbs are shown in the style so typical of the Northwest Coast region. The eyes are large sections of abalone shell. The trim is a buckskin strip decorated with puffin beaks and deer-hoof rattles.

HAIDA   20 × 30 in.   1825–1850
American Museum of Natural History: 16/344

127 *Dance Apron*

Made of painted buckskin, aprons of this style were worn by shamans in ceremonial dances. Various decorations were added, such as carvings, fur, cloth or leather appliqués. The designs usually represented spirits of mythological beings who were called upon to assist the shaman in curing a patient. A flannel trim is sewn to the hem of this apron, to which puffin beaks and deer hoofs have been fastened to serve as rattles.

TLINGIT; Cape Fox, Alaska   27 × 40 in.   1850–1875
Washington State Museum: 1956

128 *Man's Shirt*

Such woven garments were worn by wealthy individuals, and the designs usually indicated their genealogical background. The design technique shows the subject in a combined X-ray and split-open fashion; careful examination reveals the front and both sides of the animal. Woven from goat hair on a cedar-bark base, these are the same in style, coloring, and basic technique as the garment shown in Plate 129.

TLINGIT; Alaska   L:44½ in.   1890–1900
Museum of the American Indian: 18/7902

129 *Woven Blanket*

These are worn both as shoulder blankets and as kilts or aprons. Woven from goats' wool on a shredded cedar-bark base, they are the best-known textile from the Northwest Coast region. Usually these are known as "Chilkat blankets," after the sub-tribe which specialized in their weaving. The complicated pattern is actually a view of the Brown Bear as seen from the front and both sides; the various portions of his anatomy are treated in a very abstract style. This specimen was collected in 1907 by Lt. G. T. Emmons.

TLINGIT; Cape Prince of Wales, Alaska   W:64 in.   1850–1875
Museum of the American Indian: 9/7438

130 *Movable Wooden Doll*

A great variety of puppet-type dolls are used throughout the Northwest Coast region. This fine carving has a head which can be manipulated at will; some dolls are even more movable, with hinged limbs and rotating eyes. The "hair" on this specimen is a patch of sealskin. At first glance the outsize hands seem awkward; study reveals surprising grace and balance in the proportions of this figurine, which was collected in England, where it had been taken many years ago.

NOOTKA; Vancouver, British Columbia   H:19 in. 1825–1875
Museum of the American Indian: 19/6189

131 *Wooden Mask*

The feeling of Makah wood carving is different from that of many neighboring tribes; they usually utilize a rather low-relief technique. This mask was originally painted in various colors, which have faded with age, a loss which serves further to emphasize the carving.

MAKAH; Neah Bay, Washington   H:13 in.   1850–1890
Museum of the American Indian: 1/9514

132 *Wooden Figurine*

This effigy is carved at the upper end of a shaman's staff, and represents his spirit helper. The painting and design have a very modern quality. Deer-hoof rattles are tied to the figure to provide rhythm when the staff is shaken during ceremonies.

QUINAULT; Washington   Figure: 7½ × 15½ in.   1890–1900
American Museum of Natural History: 16A/4921

133 *Mother and Child*

This remarkable piece of Salish woodcarving is particularly interesting in that it demonstrates the technique of head-flattening practiced by these people. The child is securely bound in the cradle, then the head is so wrapped as to eventually elongate the skull in the admired fashion. Collected from the Saanetch people in 1927 by Lt. G. T. Emmons.

SONGISH; Vancouver, British Columbia   H:16 in. 1875
Museum of the American Indian: 15/4413

Wooden Dance Mask

Representing *Swaixwe*, the mythical Sky Being who came down to earth and lives in lakes, this mask is used in a social dance performed by specific people privileged to enact the role. In use, the mask has a collar of swan feathers and is topped by a fringe of sea lion whiskers; the birds are hooded mergansers. The ability of the artist to incorporate a variety of elements into a single design is clearly demonstrated—note how the **three** bird's heads form an integrated composition. Compare this mask with the one in Plate 90.

COWICHAN; Vancouver, British Columbia   H:20 in. 1890–1900
Museum of the American Indian: 18/1062

134 *Adze and Handle*

Implements of this form were used for most of the woodcarving done by these people. The metal blade of this adze was obtained by trade from the white man; in earlier days such blades were of stone or jadeite. The whalebone handle of this specimen is carved to represent the seagull.

QUILEUTE; Washington   L:10½ in. 1850–1900
Museum of the American Indian: 5/7552

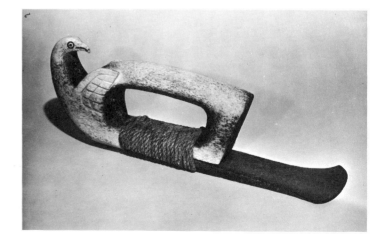

135

136 *Shaman's Board*

Little is known about these *Tamanus* boards, of which this is perhaps the only surviving example. They are believed to represent a shaman's "power board," which was deposited near his grave and left to disintegrate. To the artist, the important feature was the face, and the balance of the figure is only casually suggested. The whole concept is in keeping with other Salish carving, and the emphasis upon the planes of the face has an interesting similarity to certain Melanesian art forms. The eyes are inlaid shell.

SALISH; Bay Center, Washington   28 × 78 in.   1890–1900
American Museum of Natural History: 16/6946

137 *Horn Ladle*

These are made by boiling mountain-sheep horn to soften it, opening it out sufficiently to achieve the desired shape, and then carving it. Compare the art style with that of the human figure in Plate 139 and of the "ribbed" animal in Plate 5; the same emphasis on skeletal structure is common to all of these.

WASCO; The Dalles, Oregon   L:9½ in.   1850–1875
Museum of the American Indian: 3196

138 *Ceremonial Rattle*

This rattle is made from mountain-sheep horn boiled and flattened into sheets for fashioning. The wrapping is native-spun wool. The design represents *Swaixwe,* the Sky Being, and is used in dances by the performer playing this part and also in naming ceremonies. See Plate 135.

SALISH; Vancouver, British Columbia   L:13½ in.   1890–1900
Museum of the American Indian: 20/347

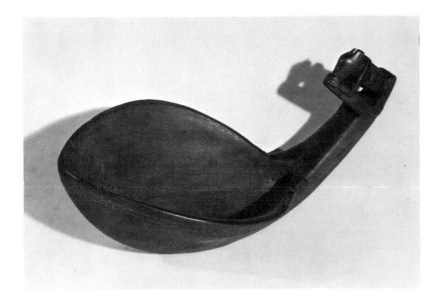

139 *Twined Bag*

Made by twining Indian hemp over the warp base, these flexible cylinder baskets are woven in a variety of sizes. The designs are characteristic of this tribe, and portray the human form in an unusual skeletonlike technique. The upper pair of figures is male, while the lower two are female.

WASCO; Oregon   H:12 in.   1880–1900
Museum of the American Indian: 8633

140 *Bark Box and Cover*

This article is made from birch bark, with the peeled-bark designing typical of this tribe. A great variety of functional forms are made from this material and decorated with animal and plant forms.

MONTAGNAIS; Quebec, Canada   H:5½ in.   1900
Museum of the American Indian: 2/8833

141 *Quilled Pouch*

While North American tribes in general created a veritable art form from the lowly porcupine quill, the people of western Canada developed the use of quills to the ultimate. A comparison of this pouch quilled on elkskin with the other examples in Plates 242 and 248 clearly demonstrates the technical superiority of the more northerly tribes. Both sewn and woven quill techniques were familiar to these workers, and almost all costumes and similar objects were so decorated.

CHIPEWYAN; Lake Athabasca, Canada   L:10½ in.   1875–1900
Museum of the American Indian: 5/3105

142 *Knife Sheath*

This is a particularly fine example of a style of quillwork which is unique to the western Canada tribes. These people are unsurpassed in their use of finely split porcupine and bird quills.

CHIPEWYAN; Lake Athabasca, Canada   L:9 in. 1840
Museum of the American Indian: 19/4548

143 *Polychrome Basket*

This striking design in a fine weave is characteristic of the excellent work produced by this little-known tribe. Never numerous, these people have managed to create masterpieces of basketry while inhabiting an arid, barren region—truly a triumph of man over environment.

PANAMINT; California   H:8 in. 1900
University Museum: NA 8279

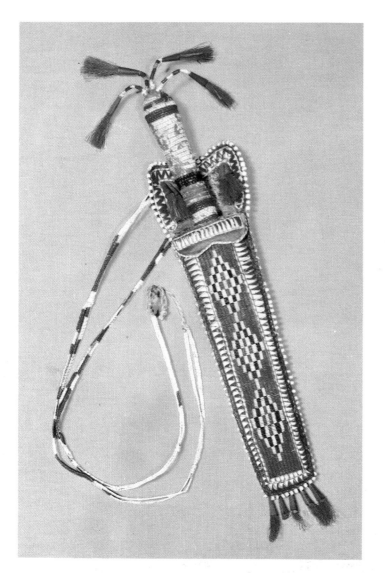

144 *Woman's Legging*

Made from caribou skin and painted in the traditional style, these were fastened just below the knee and worn with a long overgarment. The design is similar to that seen all through the Northeast, and is repeated in bark, bead, and quill work. This example was collected in Labrador and taken to England sometime before 1840.

NASKAPI; Labrador, Canada   L:17½ in. 1800–1840
Museum of the American Indian: 3/2901

145 *Polychrome Basket*

Some of the least impressive cultures produce surprising artwork. The civilization manifested by this small tribe may seem impoverished, yet the quality of tribal weaving is equal to that of the best Western basketmakers.

CHEMEHUEVI; California   H:5½ in. 1900
University Museum: NA 8804

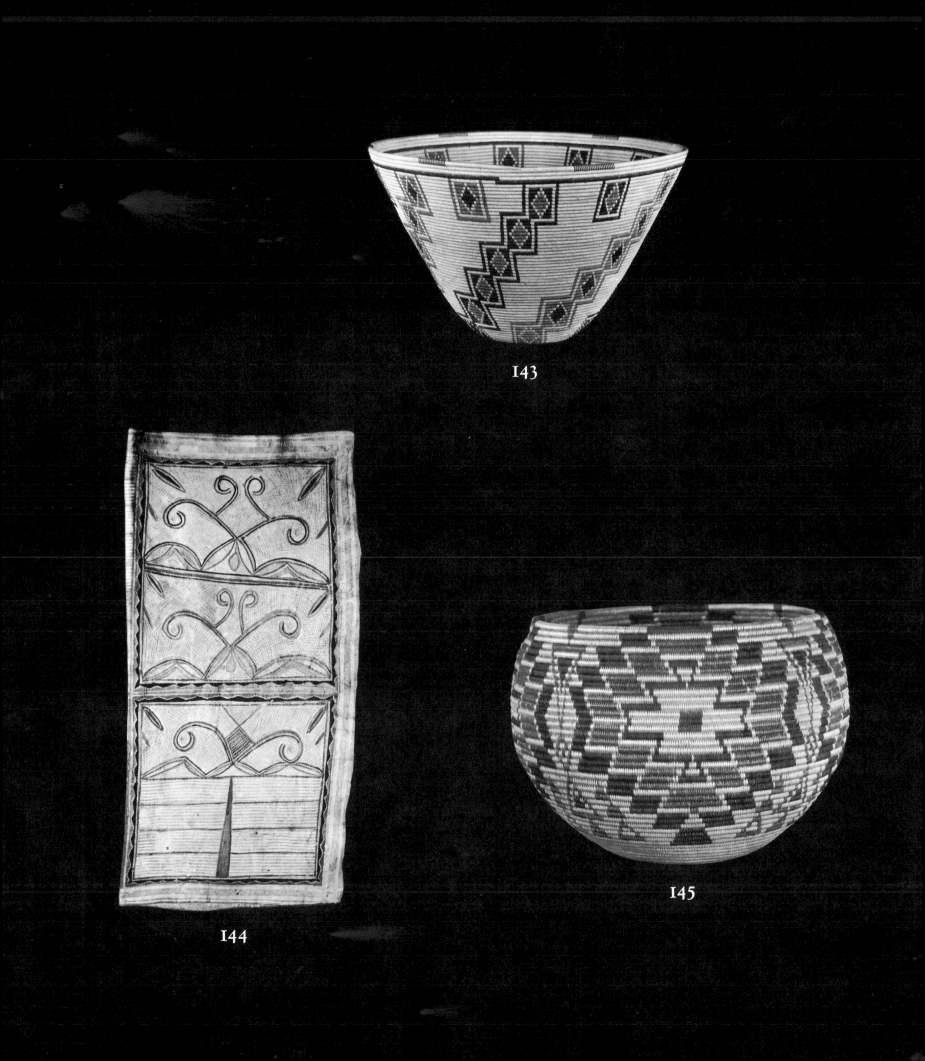

143

144

145

146 *Gift Basket*

This finely woven basket is made of black maidenhair fern and yellow-dyed quills. Although such baskets adhere fully to the old-time techniques in materials and manufacture, covered baskets of this general shape and design were made to meet the demands of white purchasers. This was woven by Mrs. Hickox.

KAROK; California   H:8 in. 1900–1925
Museum of the American Indian: 16/3589

147 *Gambling Tray*

Finely woven trays of this design were customarily used for the men's gambling game in which a set of nutshell dice were thrown onto the tray. The design representing men dancing in a circle, surrounding a large coiled rattlesnake, is typical of the work of Lake Tulare weavers.

YOKUTS; California   D:31 in. 1875–1900
University Museum: NA 8307

148 *Willow Basket*

This superb basket is one of the finest existing examples of the work of Datsolali, a famed Washo weaver. Few basketmakers attained the position where their names became familiar and collectors sought their products; this example shows why Datsolali reached that eminence. The weave of this basket is thirty stitches to the inch, and eleven months were required to finish it. The design was called "We Assemble to Discuss the Happy Lives of Our Ancestors" by the maker—eloquent proof of the difficulty of translating Indian symbolism into English concepts. It is from the famous Clark Field collection.

WASHO; Nevada   13 × 52 in. 1918
Philbrook Art Center: MI 3199

149 *Effigy Jar*

This combination of an effigy doll superimposed upon a spouted jar may be a carry-over from earlier effigy vessels which have been found in archaeological sites throughout the Southwest. These modern pieces were primarily produced for trade and for sale by both the Mohave and Yuma potters.

MOHAVE; Arizona   H:9 in.   1880–1900
Museum of the American Indian: 8/4548

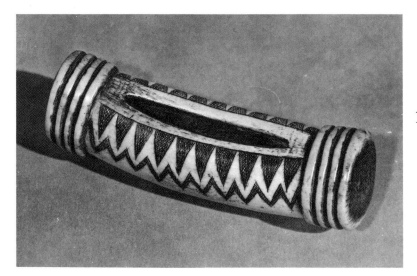

150 *Man's Purse*

These carved and incised purses made from elk antler are typical of several northern California tribes. They are used to store the dentalium-shell money which is common currency among these people. The shells are inserted in the slot, which is closed by a small bone strip fastened on with buckskin thongs.

HUPA; California   L:6 in.   1857
Museum of the American Indian: 1371

151 *Gift Basket*

Unquestionably one of the finest bead-decorated baskets in existence, this specimen has the usual woven-grass base, to which small trade beads have been added by interweaving in a strong overlay design. While such decoration of baskets by the addition of shells, beads, and feathers is typical of the tribe, few have this one's aesthetic beauty. See Plate 152.

POMO; California   4 × 12 in.   1900
Museum of the American Indian: 20/8299

152 *Feathered Gift Basket*

The soft effect of feathers against their own background is carried to its greatest heights by these weavers. While a few other Amerindians incorporate feathers into their basketry and textile art, none equal the Pomo in this regard. A similar technique was practiced by the ancient Peruvians and Polynesians. The rim is decorated with shell disk-beads, while glass beads and abalone shell pendants complete the ornamentation.

Pomo; California   H:6½ in.   1890–1910
Museum of the American Indian: 9488

153 *Pottery Dolls*

Characteristic of the southern Arizona-California area, these small dolls were used as playthings, and were popular with tourists at the turn of the century. Today they are relatively unknown and infrequently seen. They stem from a prehistoric tradition of clay figurine-making. The painted decoration represents tattooing; beads and trade cloth are used as dress accessories. Nearly identical dolls were also made by the Mohave potters, and it is almost impossible to distinguish between the work of the two tribes, particularly since intermarriage further confuses the problem.

Yuma; Arizona   H:7 in.   1880–1900
Museum of the American Indian: 21/3802, 21/3803

154 *Witchcraft Fetish Jar*

Pottery vessels of this type are kept in the *kiva*. This particular jar and the fetishes with it are used as a set by the War Chief to punish and purify witches. The bowl has a buckskin thong around the neck on which are strung pieces of turquoise, stone beads, and shells. The painted design is characteristic of Zuñi pottery art of the period. The zoömorphic fetishes are carved from elk and deer antler, and are decorated with turquoise, shell, feathers, and buckskin. When not in use, they are housed in the vessel and are "fed" sacred corn meal through the circular hole in the side.

ZUÑI; New Mexico   H: 9½ in.   1850–1900
Museum of the American Indian: 20/3696

155 *Water Jar*

Although the deer and fawns painted on this vessel are normal for the period, the decoration is unusual, for it departs from the traditional zoning of Zuñi pottery art. All-over animal patterns are not common in Pueblo art. This specimen was collected in 1880 by Douglas C. Graham, the first Indian agent at Zuñi Pueblo.

ZUÑI; New Mexico   H:10 in.   1880
Museum of the American Indian: 22/7882

156 *Water Vessel*

This is a fine example of the quality of ceramics now fast disappearing from Acoma Pueblo. At one time such vessels were made regularly, both for use and for sale, and were held in high esteem by pottery connoisseurs. Today there are fewer than a half-dozen competent potters in the village. The design on this specimen is quite different from the typical work from this pueblo, which is more commonly expressed in floral or animalistic motifs.

ACOMA; New Mexico   H:9½ in.   1890–1910
Museum of the American Indian: 19/4333

157 *Pottery Vessel*

Some of the finest Pueblo pottery of recent times comes from the Hopi, and this is an example of superior ceramic design in which the clean-line pattern indicates a sure hand and the precise composition for which these potters are noted. As in all North American Indian art, no potter's wheel was used to achieve the shape of this vessel; the maker used only her hands and a few shaping and polishing stones.

HOPI; Arizona   H:20 in.   1890
Museum of the American Indian: 19/2701

158 *Feather Belt*

Woven on a milkweed-fiber base, this belt was worn across one shoulder by men. In ancient times women wove these ceremonial belts; the present example was made by Charles Benson, a Pomo man who kept the art alive for a time. No two of these designs are made alike; aside from their decorative and symbolic importance, they are thought to possess a magical power to frighten enemies. Featherwork of the same technique was also produced in ancient Peru, Hawaii, and among the Maori peoples.

POMO; California   5½ × 68 in.   1875–1900
Museum of the American Indian: 16/984

159 *Pottery Vessel*

This is a typical specimen of the blackware pottery developed by the famed Julián and María Martínez, who brought about a renaissance in Pueblo pottery in the 1920's. Their work is distinguished by simple, carefully modeled forms, decorated with crisp, clean matte designs on a highly polished background. This jar bears a repeat pattern of feathers.

SAN ILDEFONSO; New Mexico   H:8 in.   1925-1950
Collection of Dr. and Mrs. Frederick J. Dockstader

160 *Woman's Shawl*

This finely woven textile was made with hand-spun wool, and exhibits the best in women's wear of the mid-1800's. Garments of this type were worn as shawls over a regular wool dress. Their use went out in the early 1900's, and today they are no longer made

NAVAJO; Arizona   36 × 51 in.   1875-1890
Museum of the American Indian: 11/8069

161 *Woven Blanket*

This fine example of Navajo textile artistry is woven in what is commonly termed the "chief's blanket" design, although this pattern never had such a restricted use. It is true, however, that such a blanket was intended for a man; women's blankets of this type had narrower striping. An interesting feature is that if carefully woven, the basic pattern remains the same even when the blanket is folded in quarters.

NAVAJO; Arizona   52 × 62 in.   1880–1900
Museum of the American Indian: 21/4885

162 *Basketry Tray*

This maze design is called *Siuhū Ki,* and represents the house of *Siuhū,* who figures in several Pima legends. He lived far in the mountains, where trails became so confused that no one could follow him. Made from natural undyed plant materials, these trays rarely serve native uses, but are primarily intended for sale.

PIMA; Sacatón, Arizona   D:9½ in.   1900–1915
Museum of the American Indian: 11/415

163 *Wicker Plaque*

These flat trays are used as gifts, decorations in the home, and for carrying corn meal in ceremonies. Woven from grasses dyed in various colors, the technique has been practiced for centuries by the Hopi and their prehistoric ancestors. Today the plaques are popular with non-Indians for use as gifts and as wall decorations. The variety of designs used is almost endless.

HOPI; Oraibi, Arizona   D:14 in.   1935
Collection of Dr. and Mrs. Frederick J. Dockstader

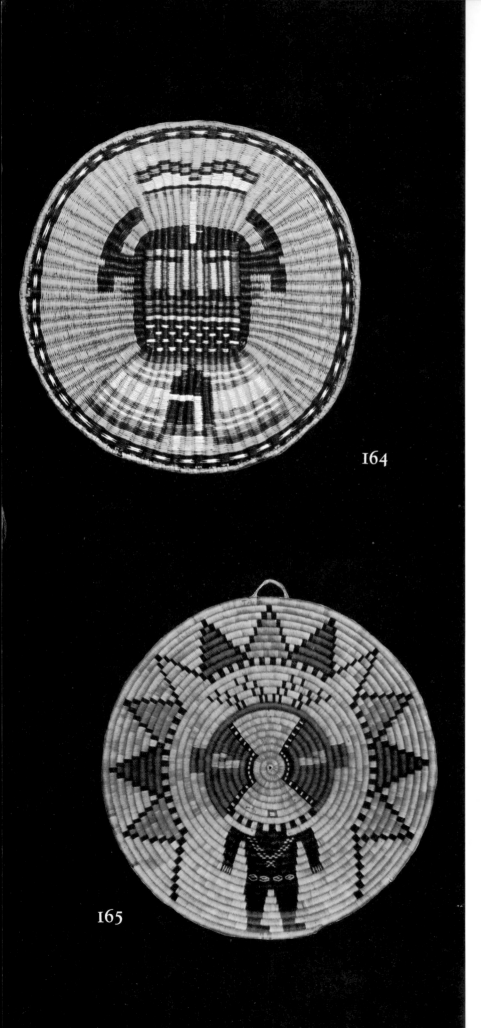

164

165

164 *Wicker Plaque*

This technique is peculiar to the Western, or Third Mesa weavers, and is quite different from that practiced in the central Hopi villages, as illustrated in Plate 165. The various designs employed in these flat plaques include birds, animals, and humans. This portrayal of *Hūmis Kachina Mana* depicts her mask and the traditional "maiden's whorls" of her coiffure.

HOPI; Oraibi, Arizona   D:16 in.   1940
Museum of the American Indian: 18/972

165 *Basketry Plaque*

Coiled weaving of this particular style is made only at the Second Mesa villages, and closely resembles a basketry technique popular in North Africa. No other Amerindian tribe makes basketry of this type. The design represents a masked being—*Kipok Kachina,* the Warrior. He is shown wearing his mask, a silver necklace, and a silver concha belt. In early days these served as food trays; today they are primarily made for sale.

HOPI; Shungopovi, Arizona   D:15 in.   1925
Museum of the American Indian: 17/9661

166 *Woolen Blanket*

In the early days of Navajo weaving, women obtained English red baize, or *bayeta,* unraveled and respun it for use in some of their finest textiles. These tightly woven blankets are highly prized by collectors today. This fine example of *bayeta* weaving was collected about 1884, and has an interesting repeat pattern in simple red, black, gray, and white colors.

NAVAJO; New Mexico   33 × 54 in.   1880–1884
Museum of the American Indian: 6/1088

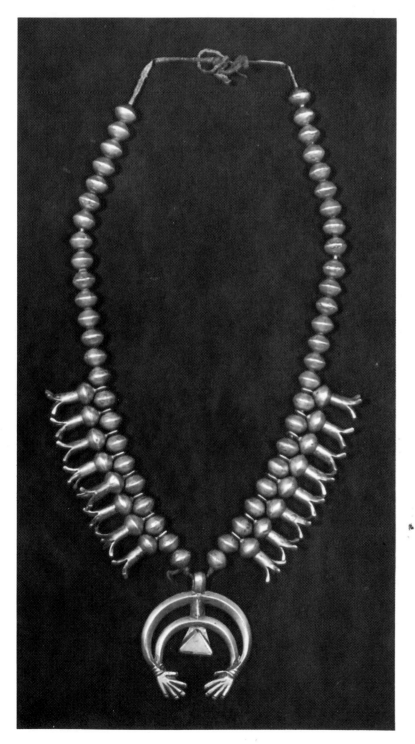

167 *Silver Necklace*

This design, the so-called "squash blossom" necklace, was adapted from colonial Mexican costume decoration of the early 1800's. The pendant, or *naja,* is adapted from bridle ornaments of the same era, which were used to ward off the evil eye. These necklaces have become so widespread in the Southwest that many people erroneously believe them to be a "traditional" Indian design. In recent years this simple jewelry has become so overburdened with turquoise that it has lost much of its aesthetic effectiveness. See Plate 171.

NAVAJO; Arizona   L:15 in.   1920
Museum of the American Indian: 6/2128

168 *Silver Wrist Guard*

The design for such a bow guard is first carved on a flat sandstone surface, and then molten silver is poured into the mold. After finishing, turquoise is mounted in the cups, and the ornament is fastened to a leather wristlet. Originally the *ketoh* was used to protect the archer's wrist from the bowstring; today it is worn as personal adornment. The design varies somewhat, but usually adheres fairly consistently to this form, called a "spider design" because of the radiating limbs.

NAVAJO; New Mexico $3\frac{1}{2} \times 4\frac{1}{2}$ in.   1920
Museum of the American Indian: 19/999

169 "Fresh Trail, Apache War Party" by Allan Houser

This fine water color is by the foremost Apache artist living today, who is widely known for his mural paintings. The scene represents an old-time war party following the trail.

APACHE; Arizona
Philbrook Art Center: IPC/575

22 × 35 in. 1952

170 *War Shield*

Like most Indians, the Apache warriors used shields to a great extent. This buckskin specimen portrays a representation of the owner's *tipi* beneath a blazing sun. To the left is a medicine bird, perhaps an eagle. The triangles and forked lines are mountains and trees. Such art is true symbolism, and the actual meaning can be interpreted only by the maker.

APACHE; New Mexico   D:19 in.   1860–1880
Museum of the American Indian: 10/8191

171 *Silver Bridle*

Beautiful horses' bridles of this simple design were made by native smiths after patterns common in Spanish bridles of the period. They were fitted with an iron bit, usually of Mexican manufacture. This particular specimen is of interest in that it was made by Atsidi Chon, one of the very first Navajo smiths. The decoration was achieved by incising or engraving with a file, a method which predates the used of stamped designs in which dies were used. The crescentic ornament on the forehead is the forerunner of the "squash blossom" necklace ornament, or *naja*, shown in Plate 167. This was collected in 1880.

NAVAJO; New Mexico   L:17½ in.   Before 1880
Museum of the American Indian: 22/8176

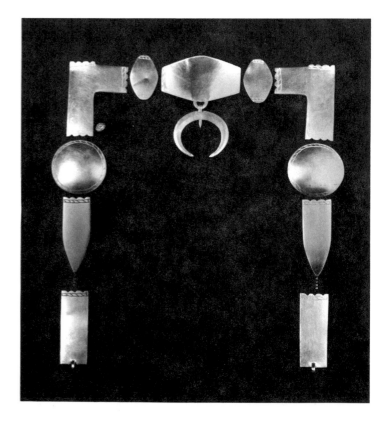

172 *Dance Headdress*

These beautifully decorated wooden boards are fastened to a wood-and-leather cap, and are worn by women during the Corn Dance. The black wig is dyed sheep's wool, and black horsehair "bangs" drop over the eyes of the dancer. The designs symbolize the sun, moon, stars, clouds, and rain. Collected by Frederick Webb Hodge in 1915.

Zuñi; New Mexico   H:35 in.   1915
Museum of the American Indian: 10/8739

173 *Fiddle and Bow*

With the possible exception of the musical bow, no stringed instrument is known to have been used by the North American Indian in pre-Columbian times. This type of violin was adapted by the Apache from European prototypes, and has been in use by them for perhaps a hundred years. The sound box is a yucca stalk, hollowed out and painted in a variety of decorative designs. The bow is of horsehair.

WHITE MOUNTAIN APACHE; Arizona   L:24 in.   1920
Museum of the American Indian: 20/7147

174 *War God Statue*

Representing *Ahayuta,* one of the Twin War Gods of the Zuñi such figurines are carved and placed in the War Shrine following traditional ceremonies. They are then allowed to disintegrate. The cap on this figure is the ancient knitted cotton helmet; a feather normally projects from the peak. The hair is an exaggerated stylization of the regular Zuñi coiffure; the body is completely stylized. The horizontal shaft represents a feather cylinder which is the figure's umbilicus. By extension, in Zuñi legend, this represents the *Sipapu,* or Center of Life, the Place of Emergence. The horizontally cut ridges represent the hands of the War God. Pieces of this quality are extremely rare, since they normally decay rapidly. This one, collected in 1920, is among the finest known.

ZUÑI; New Mexico   L:27½ in.   1900–1920
Collection of Dr. and Mrs. Frederick J. Dockstader

175 *Wooden Figurine*

This figurine represents the *Shálako Mana,* who appears with her mate in the rarely seen Shálako ceremonies. The full costume worn by this personator is shown in Plate 183. This fine example of early Hopi figurine art was collected by Charles Day before 1900; later examples added the eagle-feather costuming and often were extremely ornate. The painted headdress of this figure bears designs symbolic of various weather and agricultural features important to the tribe.

HOPI; Oraibi, Arizona   H:25 in.   1880–1900
Museum of the American Indian: 3709

176 *Kachina Figurine*

This figurine represents *Kwahū Kachina,* the Eagle Being. It is not to be confused with the "Eagle Dancers" frequently seen at social or commercial entertainments. While the continuity of Kachina art is unbroken from prehistoric times, many technical innovations have been introduced; today there is much greater emphasis placed upon sculptural realism than in former times. Compare this fine example of contemporary Hopi sculpture with the more traditional static pose shown in Plate 184.

HOPI; Shungopovi, Arizona   H:11 in.   1956
Museum of the American Indian: 22/6266

177 *Kachina Figurine*

Representing *Tselele Kachina,* this illustrates the typical Zuñi Kachina doll. It differs from the Hopi figurines largely in the use of realistic costumes, detached arms, and a much more angular body proportion. Zuñi work is usually less well carved but more elaborately decorated. The tribal function of these figurines is much the same as with the Hopi, but since the Zuñi rarely make theirs for sale, they are much less commonly seen.

ZUÑI; New Mexico   H:17 in.   1900–1910
Brooklyn Museum: 5351

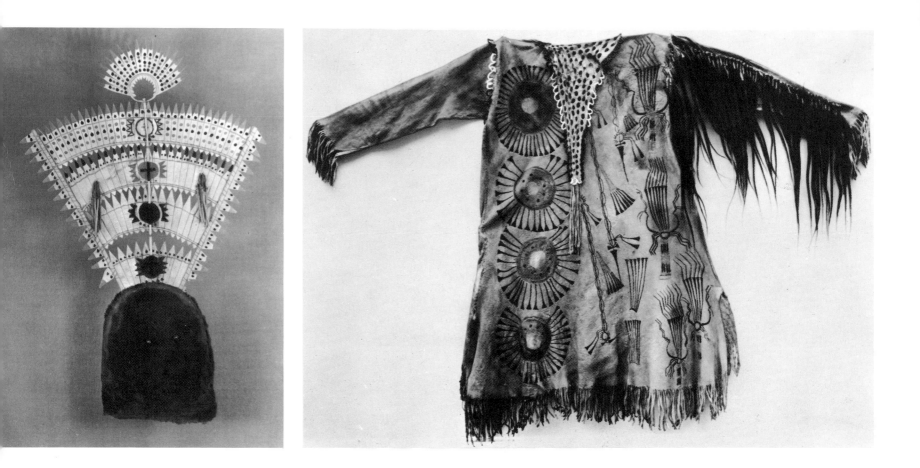

178 *Dance Headdress*

Worn by the *Gan* Dancers, commonly called Devil Dancers, these yucca-slat pieces have no standard decoration, for they are painted by the performer as the mood strikes. The ceremony in which they are used is in celebration of the puberty rites of a maiden, quite similar to the debut of a young girl in contemporary society. It is a powerfully dramatic performance enhanced by rhythmic music, masked figures, and these striking headdresses. In former times the mask was made of buckskin; today, trade cloth is universal.

SAN CARLOS APACHE; Arizona   H:37 in. 1915
Museum of the American Indian: 8/9949

179 *Painted Shirt*

The composition and technical execution of the decoration on this buckskin garment reveals considerable aesthetic ability; shirts of such superior quality are rare. The strands of human hair are commonly called "scalp locks," but they do not represent individual scalps in most instances—one scalp often provided enough hair for a dozen such locks. Although collected in 1850 by Thomas S. Twiss, Indian agent at Fort Laramie, and attributed by him to the Apache, the design, style, and cut of the garment suggest a more likely Northern Plains origin.

CHIRICAHUA APACHE; Arizona (?)   L:31 in. 1850
Museum of the American Indian: 8/8017

180 *Kachina Mask*

Of painted buckskin, trimmed in horsehair, this represents *Itetsipona Kachina*, the Double Face Being, and shows the typical face mask of this tribe. The relationship between the Zuñi and Hopi masked beings is extremely close. The beard is of feathers and black horsehair.

ZUÑI; New Mexico   L:14 in.   1905
Museum of the American Indian: 12/765F

181 *Dance Wand*

Carried in the hand by women dancers, these painted boards are made in pairs, with various symbols. This *mánayawi* contains designs representing a *Qŏcha Kachina* mask surmounting a rainbow and symbolic clouds, and a stylized ear of corn at the base. It was made from a pine wood slat; earlier examples were of yucca wood.

HOPI; Oraibi, Arizona   L:24 in.   1890
Museum of the American Indian: 9/572

182 *Kachina Dance Mask*

The mask represents *Sio Hūmis Kachina*. The elaborate headdress is made of canvas stretched over a wooden frame, painted and decorated with feathers. The cylindrical mask itself is made of heavy leather. When in use, a collar of evergreen conceals the bottom edge of the mask. The variety of Hopi Kachina beings cannot be accurately established; well over 350 different personages have been tentatively identified. Collected by H. R. Voth in 1895.

HOPI; Oraibi, Arizona   H:22 in.   1895
Museum of the American Indian: 18/6295

F. Kabotie

183 *"The Shálako People" by Fred Kabotie*

This painting by Fred Kabotie depicts three major participants in the Hopi *Shálako* ceremony: the *Shálako, Hahaí-i Wūqti,* and the *Shálako Mana.* These huge feathered costumes, surmounted by great masks and headdresses, are carried by a performer hidden inside each figure. Although this ritual was adopted from the neighboring Zuñi people, the Hopi have added considerable elaboration to the costuming. See Plate 175.

HOPI; Oraibi, Arizona   15 × 20 in.   1930
Museum of the American Indian: 18/2058

184 *Kachina Doll*

Representing *Ho-ole Kachina,* this is typical of the standard "Kachina Doll" most commonly seen today. The painting and form have been stylized, but the basic elements by which the Kachina may be identified are retained. Although such wooden dolls are primarily made for sale, they are also given to the young children at ceremonies to aid them in learning to identify the various masked beings.

HOPI; Oraibi, Arizona   H:10 in.   1950
Collection of Dr. and Mrs. Frederick J. Dockstader

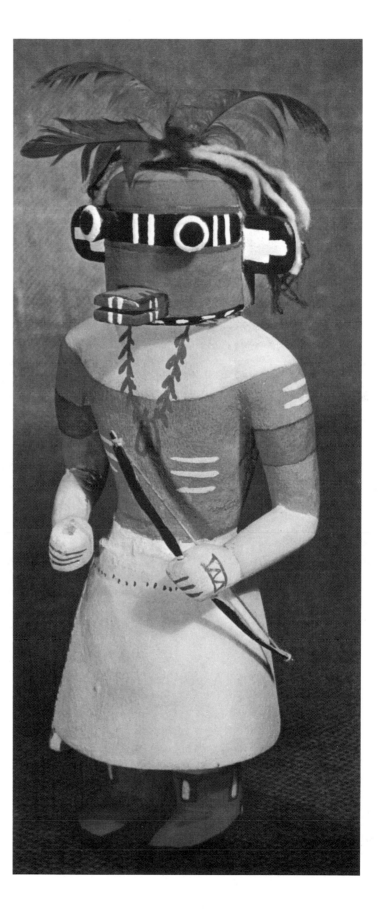

185 *Woven Bag (front)*
186 *Woven Bag (rear)*

These plates illustrate both sides of the same specimen. Such bags are commonly made throughout the Plateau area, and the technique is so similar that accurate tribal identification is often impossible. It is of interest to note that the designs are almost never the same on both sides of the bags and that they usually have no relationship to each other. This twined weave is achieved by wrapping cornhusk or rush around the weft in a false embroidery technique. See also Plates 227 and 228.

NEZ PERCÉ; Idaho   L:22 in. 1885–1900
Museum of the American Indian: 12/2433

187 *"Two Weavers" by Harrison Begay*

One of the best-known Navajo artists, Harrison Begay has done many murals, and is perhaps as well known in this field as Allan Houser. This example of his work is characteristic of his whole style. *Photograph by Bob McCormack.*

NAVAJO; Arizona   25 × 34 in. 1946
Philbrook Art Center: IPC/615

188 *"In the Days of the Plentiful"*
by Quincy Tahoma

This spirited action painting shows Quincy Tahoma's work at its best. His skill with horses and movement is outstanding among Indian artists. *Photograph by Martin Wiesendanger.*

NAVAJO; Arizona   28 × 37½ in.   1946
Philbrook Art Center: IPC/596

189 *Kachina Mask*

This represents *Hemüshikwe Kachina*, the Earth and Sky Being, one of the most colorful of the Zuñi Kachinas. In use, the leather mask has a flat painted tablet fastened to the head and elaborate feather decorations, with a spruce collar around the neck. A comparison with the Hopi adaptation of this same design is offered in Plate 182; such ceremonial interchange was common throughout the Southwest. Collected by Frederick Webb Hodge.

ZUÑI; New Mexico   W:8 in.   1925
Museum of the American Indian: 12/764F

190 *"Ceremonial Buffalo Dance"* *by Velino Herrêra*

The artist has this to say about his painting: "As in all animal dances, this is given to appease the spirits of the animals that have been killed, so they will return in great numbers. This religious ceremony is usually held during the winter or early spring, and lasts four days. The dancers imitate the hunt; in this painting are deer and antelope dancers as well as buffalo. The chorus sings an effective song, and the participants also include the Old Man, the various animals and the Buffalo Mother."

ZIA; New Mexico   21 × 28 in. 1948
Philbrook Art Center: IPC 522

191 *Beaded Cradle Board*

An example of the elaborate cradle board favored by many of the tribes of the Basin-Plateau area. The large wooden bow protects the baby's head, and affords ample room for decoration. The child is bound into the bag of the cradle, developing a feeling of security as well as a strong, straight back.

NEZ PERCÉ; Idaho   L:37½ in. 1880
Museum of the American Indian: 18/9171

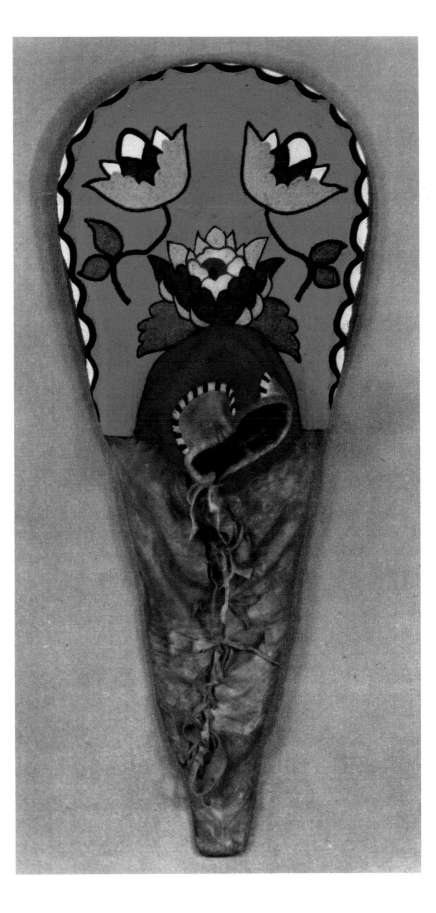

192 *Ghost Dance Shirt*

During the last desperate days of Plains resistance to the white invaders, the Ghost Dance caught the hopes of many tribes, particularly the Sioux. Shirts were painted with mystic designs believed to have supernatural power to protect the wearer against bullets; the designs were gained in visions and possessed a personal significance. Since each man painted his own shirt, the aesthetic quality of the work varies tremendously. This is painted on Government-issue muslin, as were most of these garments. See Plate 209.

SIOUX; South Dakota   L: 30 in.   1890
Museum of the American Indian: 2/9359

193 *Painted Robe*

Painted on buffalo hide, this man's robe is characteristic of one style of northwestern Plains art. The scene is a narrative of the exploits of the owner in battle. Work of this nature was always done by men. Buffalo robes of this type were customarily sewn together in the middle; the seam was hidden by the application of a long beaded "blanket strip," such as the decorative one shown.

NEZ PERCÉ; Idaho   4 × 5 ft.   1825–1875
Chicago Natural History Museum: 69143

194 *Beaded Shirt*

Solidly beaded on buckskin, shirts of this type were worn as dress-up garments by wealthy or important men. The beading was done by the man's wife as a token of her affection. She would design the work, and occasionally would endeavor to include some symbolic content in her work. Usually, however, these designs were simply decorative.

ASSINIBOIN; Saskatchewan   17 × 20½ in.   1890
Museum of the American Indian: 22/2727

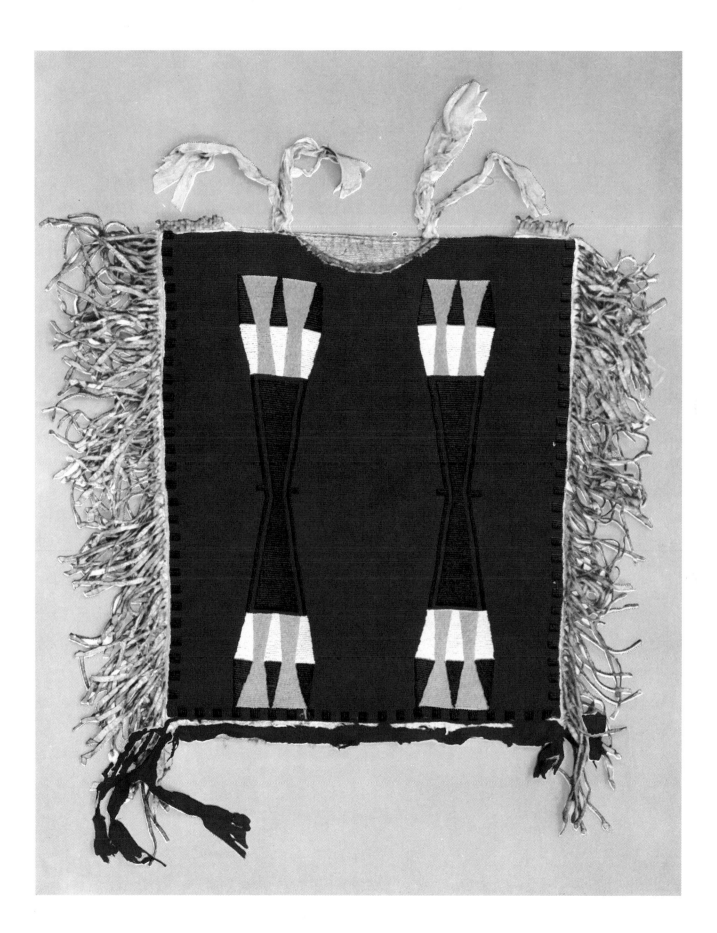

195 *War Shield and Cover*

Beneath this buckskin cover is a buffalo-hide shield which is also painted. The cover design represents a bear, which was the medicine animal of the owner, and from which he got his power. Brass bells are tied to the quills of the feather decorations. This fine example was collected in 1850 by Thomas S. Twiss, an early Indian agent at Fort Laramie.

ARIKARA; Fort Laramie, Wyoming   D:22 in.   1850
Museum of the American Indian: 8/8054

196 *War Shield Cover*

This remarkable shield painting depicts two buffalo bulls fighting. The polychrome design demonstrates the great importance placed on these articles by their owners. They were never exposed to outside gaze, and were carefully tended at all times. The painting on these shields was always done by the men.

CROW; Montana   D:20½ in.   1875
Museum of the American Indian: 2/4426

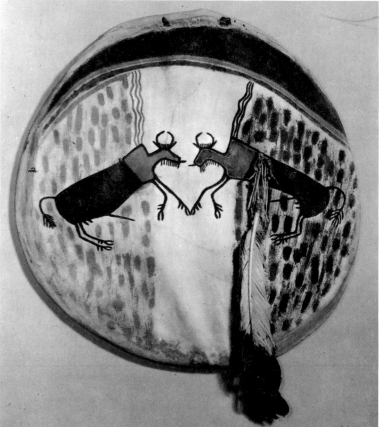

197 *Buffalo Hide Shield*

This magnificent war-medicine shield is one of the most important surviving Crow articles. It belonged to the great Chief Arapoosh at the time of the Lewis and Clark expedition. It was used as a talisman; when rolled along the ground, success was assured if it stopped face up. But if it fell face down, the project would be abandoned as foredoomed to failure. The design represents the Moon, which came to the owner in human form during a vision and gave him this shield. It was collected by William Wildschut.

CROW; Montana   D:22 in.   1800–1834
Museum of the American Indian: 11/7680

198 Beaded Horse Ornament

Such beautifully worked ornaments, beaded on buckskin, were used to adorn Crow Indian horses. This specimen was worn around the horse's neck, with the large square portion hung across the chest. The saddle and bridle were equally elaborately decorated. The red cloth was obtained from traders.

CROW; Montana   33 × 16 in.   1875–1900
Carnegie Museum: 2418/98

199 Beaded Bridle Decoration

Colorful rosettes of this design were fastened to the forehead of a horse's bridle, and were part of the fancy and elaborate horse trappings for which the Crow Indians were renowned. The wrapped circles are of yarn fastened to a buckskin base.

CROW; Montana   6 × 12½ in.   1875–1900
Carnegie Museum: 2418/97

200 Calumet

A man's pipe was one of his most important possessions, and no one touched it uninvited. It held a place of honor in his home, and everything connected with it was carefully crafted—the stem, bowl, tamper, carrying pouch, and tobacco bag. It was a religious object which the Indian regarded with great respect. This calumet stem is highly decorated with snakeskin, heads of land and water birds, feathers, and a superbly carved otter effigy bowl of catlinite. The symbolic importance of these animals was part of the personal medicine of the owner.

SIOUX; South Dakota   L:30 in.   1825–1875
Museum of the American Indian: 8756

201 *Pencil Sketch*

During the period of imprisonment following the Ghost Dance and other outbreaks, many Indians were given ledgers in which they drew various scenes to while away the time. Often these took the form of autobiographical records, the artistic quality, of course, varying with the talents of the man doing the work. This example was painted by an unknown warrior, and shows him in action.

KIOWA; Oklahoma

Collection of Mr. and Mrs. Vincent Price

$11\frac{1}{2} \times 5\frac{3}{4}$ in.   1880–1900

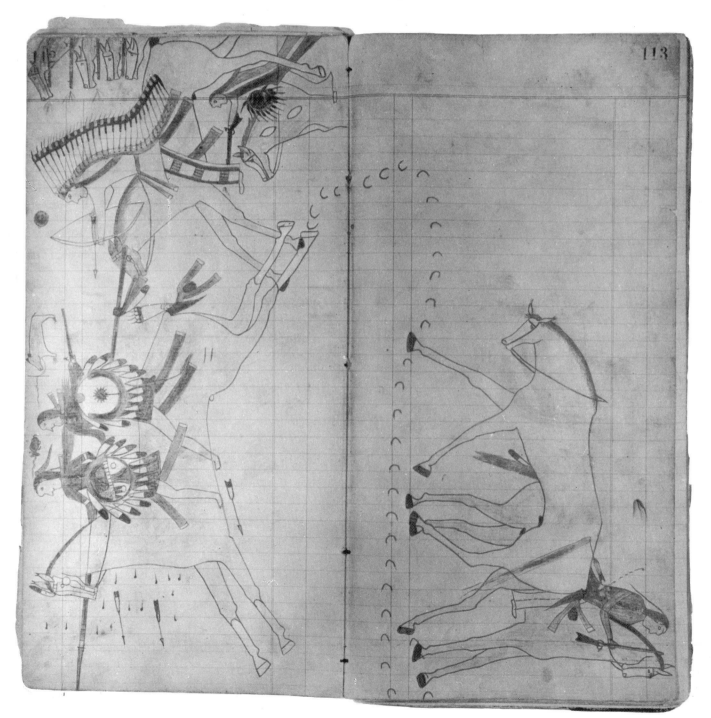

202 *Painted Shield Cover*

War shields often bore a variety of painted designs which were believed to have magic power to protect the owner. To prevent loss of this power, the shield was covered with buckskin which itself was also sometimes painted. Such painting was done by the owner, who alone knew the symbolic nature of the designs, many of which came to him in a vision. This remarkably fine buckskin cover, once the property of Pretty Bear, a Crow chief, bears designs representing the owner or his spirit protector. The crosses represent stars, and the birds are eagles. A scalp lock is suspended from one side. Collected by Charles Schreyvogel.

CROW; Montana   D:24 in.   1860
Museum of the American Indian: 20/7130

204 *Painted Hide*

This is usually called a "box design," and was reserved exclusively for use on women's robes. It is a highly stylized representation of the viscera and body proportions of a buffalo. The painting, done by women, was effected by means of a "brush" made from buffalo bone; the porous bone held the liquid paint like a sponge, and when sharpened to a fine edge, made long, neat lines. This is an exceptionally fine painting on buffalo hide.

ARAPAHO; Wyoming   69 × 96 in.   1850–1875
University Museum: 45-15-706

203 *Beaded Moccasins*

These are examples of the form and traditional design common in three northern Plains tribes; variations on these designs are almost unlimited. Each specimen has a separate hard-leather sole sewn to a soft buckskin upper. Occasionally such moccasins also had full-beaded soles; these were for extremely formal wear only, and usually were owned by wealthy members of the tribe.

SIOUX, BLACKFOOT, ASSINIBOIN   L:11½ in. max.   1808's
Museum of the American Indian: 2/9766, 4/8794, 1/467

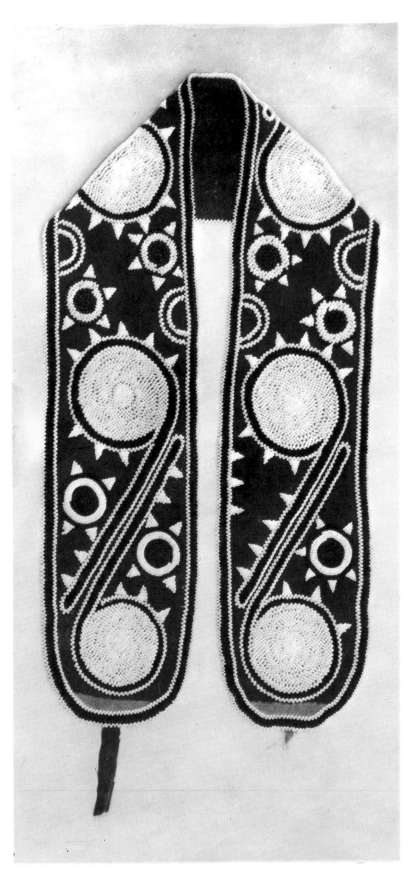

205 *Beaded Belt*

Belts with this scroll design were common to many of the Southeastern tribes, most notably the Alibamu, Koasati, Choctaw, and Creek. While the technique is not unusual, the art style is unique in that it is the only Indian beadwork pattern not affected by European design. The prehistoric ancestry of the scrollwork is clearly seen by comparison with the vessels in Plates 34 and 42.

KOASATI; Elton, Louisiana   6 × 24 in.   1825-1850
Museum of the American Indian: 1/8587

206 *Horse's Head Covering*

Made from vegetable-dyed porcupine quills on buckskin, such ornaments were used to decorate horses for show-off parades and social gatherings. While many types of horse's head coverings and masks were made by Plains tribes, such fine quilled specimens are extremely rare. Compare this with the Crow horse decorations shown in Plates 198 and 199. Collected by George B. Grinnell.

CHEYENNE; Wyoming   16 × 18 in.   1825–1875
Museum of the American Indian: 1/4443

207 *Painted Parfleche*

Made from rawhide and folded so as to hold a variety of objects, these "trunks" were common throughout the Great Plains region. This is remarkably well made, and the painted designs were carefully executed by an artistic hand. Unhappily, no data accompanies the piece, which must remain only an example of fine aesthetic merit; any tribal designation is only a guess.

PLAINS   14 × 21 in.   1875–1890
University Museum: 29-47-184

209 *Ghost Dance Dress*

This artistically painted buckskin garment belonged to the Mother of the Seven Brothers, who figure prominently in the Pawnee ritual. The designs, which she received in a vision, had a magic power to give protection and assure the efficacy of the ceremonies.

PAWNEE; Oklahoma   L:55 in.   1890–1895
Museum of the American Indian: 2/8374

208 *War Club*

Weapons of this design, made from solid wood, were used by all Eastern Woodlands people. The well-balanced form is extremely effective, and constitutes the true "tomahawk" before it was modified by the introduction of metal weapons. This especially fine old specimen bears a carved otter on the head, apparently the supernatural helper of the owner. The iron point and brass tacks came from traders. See Plate 219.

OTO; Oklahoma   L:23½ in.   1830–1850
Museum of the American Indian: 3/3555

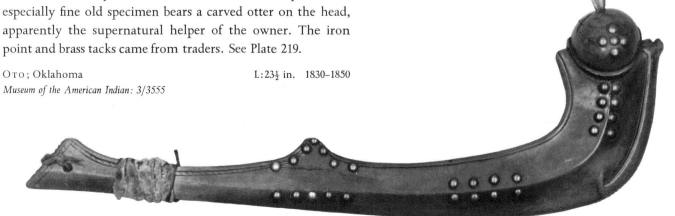

210 *Quilled Moccasins*

This is a spectacular pair of men's moccasins intended for use only on formal occasions. The base material is buffalo hide; this is decorated by dyed porcupine quills. Here the use of aniline dye results in a brilliant pattern; although the total effect is not as soft as earlier quillwork, it is nevertheless pleasing.

ARIKARA; Fort Berthold, North Dakota   L:9½ in.   1875–1900
Museum of the American Indian: 13/2818

211 *Painted Buffalo Hide*

This is a detail from a large buffalo robe. These were customarily painted by the men to narrate exploits, serve as autobiographical records, historical accounts, or to indicate the power or wealth of the owner. This robe tells of a horse-stealing raid by the owner and his friends. It is not only extremely artistic in composition and execution, but notable for the trick of indicating herds of horses by the simple expedient of painting only their heads.

CHEYENNE; Wyoming   Section: 36 × 36 in.   1850–1875
Museum of the American Indian: 16/5506

212 *Sun Dance Skull*

A bleached buffalo skull painted in traditional red and black and stuffed with prairie grass is placed on the Sun Dance altar to serve as a temporary home for the Above One during the ceremonies. It is one of the most important religious objects of the ritual, and demonstrates the Indian ability to create art from the most everyday article. The various dots each represent a prayer; black represents the earth, and red symbolizes the Arapaho tribe. The four balls of grass, corresponding to the legendary Four Old Men, indicate the days before the buffalo, when Indians wore grass clothing and Last Child was still with the people.

ARAPAHO; Wind River, Wyoming   16 × 24 in.   1900–1920
Museum of the American Indian: 13/5098

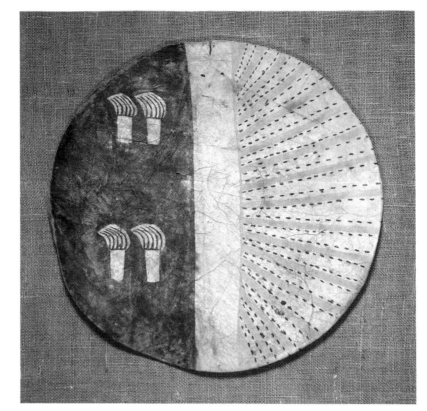

213 *War Shield*

This is a superb example of the heraldic type of shield carried by the Plains warriors at the time the white man first entered the region. The design represents four bear paws; the various lines may indicate the rays of the sun. The whole composition with its symbolic coloring is an exceptional example of balance and design harmony.

MANDAN; Upper Missouri River   D:18½ in.   Before 1850
Museum of the American Indian: 21/4017

214 *Cane Basket*

Polychrome weaving of this style is characteristic of several Southeastern peoples, but this tribe seems to have developed the greatest imagination and skill in their basketry. Made of dyed river cane, this specimen is an excellent example of the ability of the weaver to achieve a curvilinear design with a geometric weave. The art is known to have existed in prehistoric times. This more recent piece was intended primarily for sale. Collected by Dr. Margaret J. Sharpe.

CHITIMACHA; Louisiana   H:6 in.   1890
Museum of the American Indian: 22/5207

215

216

215 *Wood Effigy Figure*

The purpose of this seated figurine is not fully known, but it falls into the category of anthropomorphic spirit figures commonly used in *Midéwiwin* and related ceremonies of the Great Lakes tribes.

CHIPPEWA   H:4¾ in.   1875–1900
American Museum of Natural History: 50/3722

216 *Effigy Bowl*

Representing a beaver, this is remarkable as much for its artistic quality as for its age. Although animal effigy bowls were apparently common in earlier days, few exist today, particularly of such fine quality. This was collected in 1795, and is one of the very few specimens of Woodlands carving dating from this period.

KASKASKIA; Illinois–Indiana   4½ × 19½ in.   1750–1795
University Museum: L-83-6

217 *Feather Bonnet Case*

Rawhide cut into shape and sewn into cylindrical form was used to store feathered "war bonnets" when not in use. The bottom and top circular disks of rawhide were sewn on; the cover has a leather hinge. Such cases were made and decorated by the women; the design is characteristic of the Southern Plains region.

KIOWA; Oklahoma   H:23 in.   1850–1875
Museum of the American Indian: 11/8012

218 "*Prairie Fire*" by *Blackbear Bosin*

The artist has caught a remarkable feeling of panic, destruction, and desolation in this tempera painting.

KIOWA-COMANCHE; Oklahoma   34 × 24 in.   1953
Philbrook Art Center: IPC/381

219 *War Club*

Carved in the traditional *tómahawk* form, this is a fine example of modern Chippewa carving. While the design is more complicated than earlier examples, it is not objectionably so, and the balance and composition do no violence to the tradition of these weapons. See also Plate 208 for a more ancient example.

CHIPPEWA; Michigan   L:18¼ in.   1900
Museum of the American Indian: 12/95

220 *Medicine Bowl*

This wooden bowl, carved in one piece, is used in the *Midéwiwin* ceremonies by the individual members of that society. The bird's eyes are brass-headed tacks obtained from traders.

WINNEBAGO; Sioux City, Iowa $3\frac{1}{2} \times 2\frac{1}{2}$ in.   1850–1875
Cranbrook Institute of Science: 2249

221 *Wooden Ceremonial Bowl*

The Eastern Woodlands people used wooden bowls in a great variety of ways, and carefully carved them to bring out the beauty of the wood. Burls are frequently used for this purpose. A wide array of effigies are carved on the edges of some of the ceremonial bowls, as this illustrates. These effigies commonly represent human or animal spirits connected with the *Midéwiwin* ceremonies. Collected in 1910 by M. R. Harrington.

SAUK; Oklahoma   D: 17 in.   1860
Museum of the American Indian: 2/6544

222 *Wooden Pipe*

A further example of the versatility of the Eastern Woodlands people and their fondness for wood, this specimen is shorter than usual, and is the style often carried by men in a buckskin pouch. The beautifully worked wooden stem has lightly incised designs into which pigment has been rubbed. The catlinite bowl is inlaid with lead—an old custom among these people.

WINNEBAGO; Wisconsin   L:17½ in. 1875–1900
Museum of the American Indian: 2/3268

223 *Feather Box*

These wooden containers were used by many Woodlands tribes to store feathers for protection between ceremonies. The cover of this box bears pictographic designs which were a song record of the *Midéwiwin* ceremonies. Although they could not be read by an uninitiated person, they served to remind the singer as he chanted. Such picture writing was developed to an extremely high degree by the Chippewa, and was the closest to true writing attained in aboriginal North America.

CHIPPEWA; Wisconsin   L:20 in. 1850–1875
Museum of the American Indian: 10/6938

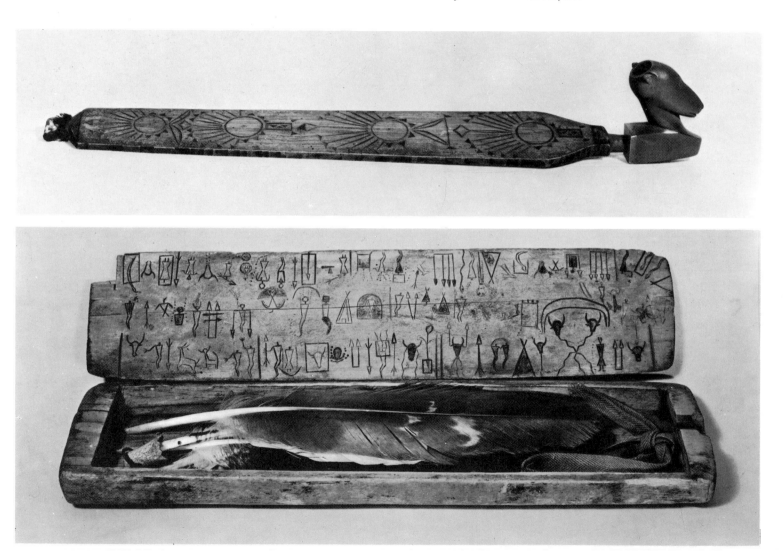

225 *Witchcraft Doll*

Part of the medicine bundle of a *Midé* Society headman, this small wooden figurine is used in Evil Medicine rites to bewitch a person. It is kept hidden in a rush mat when not in use. The eyes are brass-headed tacks; horizontal bands of red paint adorn the face. The emphasis on the carefully carved head, contrasted with the simple cylindrical body, creates a striking impression of power and forcefulness. Collected from the Berens River Salteaux by A. I. Hallowell in 1937.

CHIPPEWA; Lake Winnipeg, Manitoba   H:14 in.   1850–1900
Museum of the American Indian: 19/4960

224 *Woman's Patchwork Skirt*

Contemporary Seminole sewers have developed this art to a skilled degree. Using old-fashioned hand machines, guiding the material with one hand and cranking with the other, they sew hundreds of pieces of cotton cloth together in strips to form the patterns. While the selection of colors seems garish at first glance, the finished blend is surprisingly satisfactory. The technique is presumably adapted from mid-nineteenth century white patchwork quilting, and has become "traditional" with this tribe.

SEMINOLE; Big Cypress, Florida   L:29 in.   1956
Collection of Mrs. Alice W. Dockstader

226 *Woven Yarn Bag*

This bag was made from commercial yarn; in earlier times, native fibers were used, and spun buffalo hair was popular for such containers. The design represents the mythical Thunderbird, in repeat fashion. Such bags were used as storage for medicine bundles or personal effects, or were given as gifts at social occasions. A similar weaving technique is shown in Plate 227.

IOWA; Oklahoma   18 × 26½ in.   1880–1900
Museum of the American Indian: 2/6831

227 *Woven Yarn Bag (front)*
228 *Woven Yarn Bag (rear)*

As with Plate 226, the two sides of these yarn bags rarely bear the same design. This bag, woven from commercial yarn, depicts a group of mythical Underwater Panthers on one side, and a simple geometric pattern on the other. The zigzag lines above the Panthers represent the surface of the water. The vertical striping at either end is similar to designs woven into large mats also done by the Great Lakes tribes. Compare this with that concept in Plate 229.

MENOMINI; Wisconsin   W:22½ in.   1850-1900
Museum of the American Indian: 16/9124

229 *Quilled Medicine Pouch*

An extremely old specimen, this type of pouch was quite common in the eighteenth and nineteenth centuries. Today few exist, and this is an unusually fine example, even though it has lost its fringe of dyed deer-hair tinklers. Quilled on dyed buckskin, the pouch hints at the colorful costuming which greeted the eyes of early explorers of the Midwest. The design representing the mythical Underwater Panthers may also be seen in Plates 227 and 248.

OTTAWA; Cross Village, Michigan   6½ × 6½ in.   1800–1850
Cranbrook Institute of Science: 3690

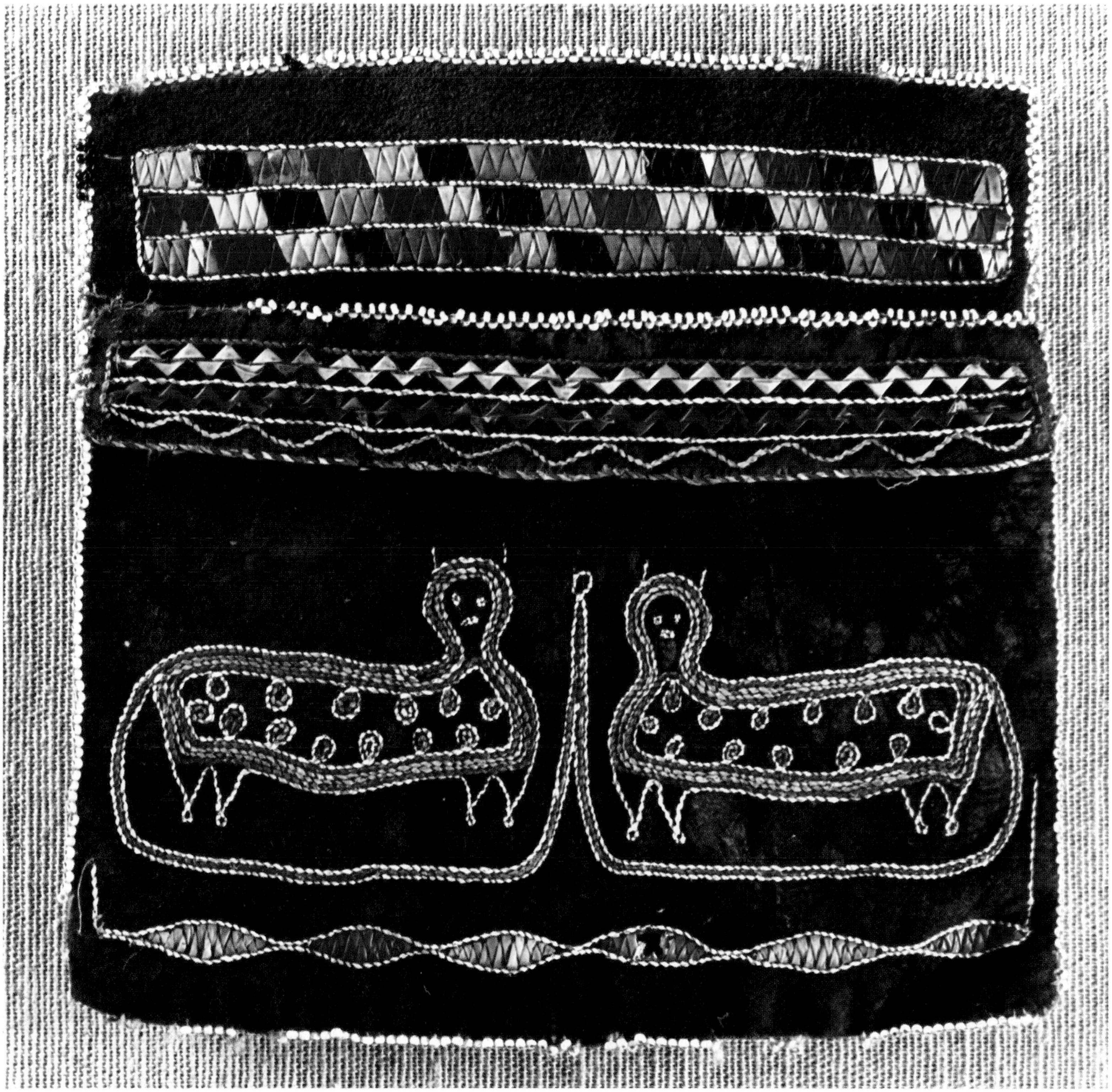

230 *Cornhusk Mask*

The Husk Face Society, also called "Bushyheads," is secondary to the wooden False Faces, and its personators must remain mute. They appear at Midwinter Festival to dance with the people and beg for food. The manufacture of such masks is based on an ancient art technique wherein cornhusks are shredded and braided. Their designs vary with the imagination of the maker, and wood features are occasionally added. This art is still actively practiced today.

SENECA; New York   D:15 in.   1910
Museum of the American Indian: 15/8349

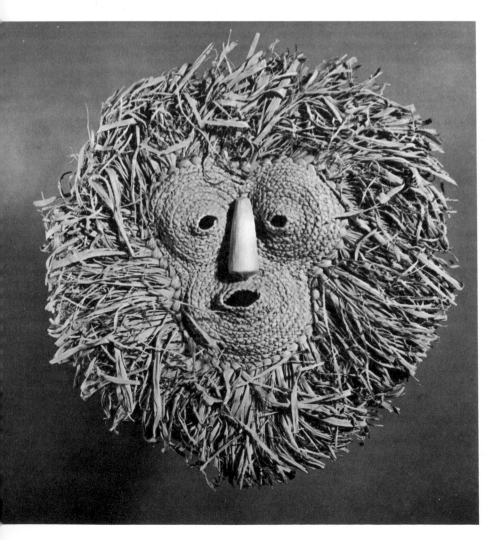

231 *Knife Sheath*

The work on this hide sheath is typical of the geometric style of Great Lakes art, as contrasted with the more common floral expression shown in Plate 247. Such sheaths were used to carry huntings or skinning knives, and were beaded (and often carried) by the women.

CHIPPEWA; Turtle Mountain, North Dakota   L:16¼ in.   1880
Museum of the American Indian: 20/4607

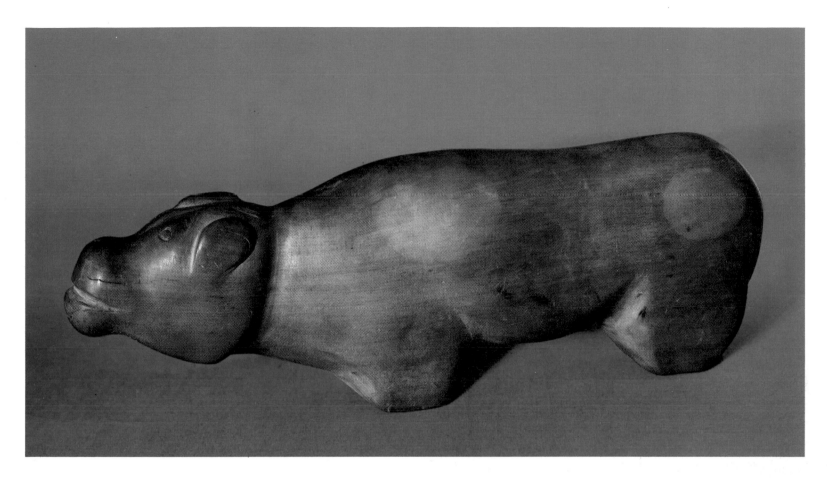

232 *Buffalo Effigy*

This carved wooden effigy is an important adjunct in the Sacred Buffalo ceremonies, and is kept with other ritual paraphernalia. It is used primarily for display when the stories of the buffalo are being narrated. This is a remarkably simple composition; such wooden pieces are extremely rare from this tribe. Collected in 1920 by Truman Michelson.

Fox; Tama, Iowa   L:18 in.   1875–1900
Museum of the American Indian: 4/7388

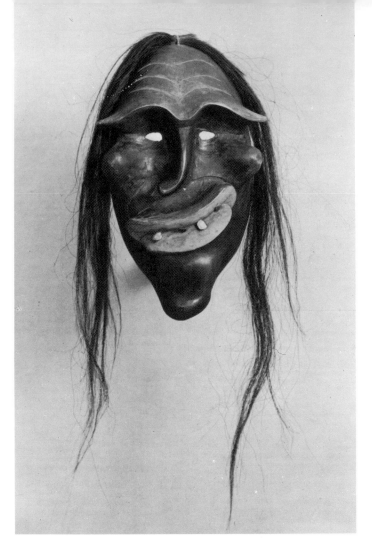

233 *Great Doctor Mask*

This is the more typical Iroquois basswood mask with horsehair trim. Representing *Hadúigona,* the Great Humpbacked One, this is the most important being in the False Face Society. Masks worn by this personator are usually seen with a twisted nose and mouth with protruding lips, portraying his pain when his face struck the mountain. The mask is exceptional for the plastic quality of the carving and the dramatic portrayal of the features. The knobbed chin is common to Onondaga and Cayuga masks, and permits the wearer to grip the mask and adjust it to his face.

ONONDAGA; New York   H:12 in.   1850–1900
Museum of the American Indian: 21/6509

234 *Harvest Mask*

Most Iroquois False Faces are not elaborately decorated. This basswood mask trimmed with horsehair is remarkable for the feather and cornhusk accessories as well as for the unusually realistic carving. At the time it was collected, it was claimed to represent the carver's expression of gratitude for a bountiful harvest. Since the identification of such masks depends mostly upon the intentions of the maker, a strict classification is not usually possible.

ONONDAGA; New York   L:34 in.; mask L:11½ in.   1875–1900
Museum of the American Indian: 6/1103

235 *Split-Body Mask*

Carved from basswood, this mask represents *Dehodiat'gaíwe*, He Whose Body is Split in Two, a being whose body is half human, half supernatural. The red and black colors symbolize east and west, or morning and afternoon (depending on when the mask was carved). Bi-colored masks are uncommon among the Iroquois, and are limited mostly to the Cayuga and Onondaga people. A similar type of bi-colored mask exists among the Delaware, and the concept may have spread to the Iroquois from that tribe. The eyes are brass grommets.

CAYUGA; Ontario, Canada   1:10¼ in.   1890
Museum of the American Indian 19/8335

236 *Woman's Shawl*

Richly embellished with silver ornaments, this is a superb example of silk ribbonwork. The technique was adapted from eighteenth-century white women's fashion, but expressed in a completely Indian manner. Garments of this quality were owned by wealthy women, and used only on formal occasions. In this illustration, the shawl is folded to show one corner.

MIAMI; Wabash, Indiana   55¼ × 55¼ in.   1825–1875
Cranbrook Institute of Science: 2208

237 *Wooden Spoon*

A magnificent example of wood carving, this unusual piece is representative of the artistic manner in which the Eastern Woodlands people decorated their utilitarian possessions. The type carried in the belt by travelers, was given to George Ellicott in 1799 by Chief Tarhe, the greatest of the Wyandot leaders.

WYANDOT; Upper Sandusky, Ohio   L:8½ in.   1799
Museum of the American Indian: 14/9600

238 *Wooden War Club*

An early example of a *tómahak* with a metal blade, this is notable not only for the fine incised decoration, but for its well-proportioned handle. The design shows an Indian using just such a weapon—perhaps the owner of this very specimen, showing off his prowess? The manner in which the design has been adapted to form a fish is unique.

MAHICAN; Massachusetts   L:22 in.   Before 1800
Museum of the American Indian: 20/2196

239 *Woman's Robe*

Garments of this design were made to serve as skirts, robes, and shawls, depending upon the size and cut. This is a superb example of ribbonwork in which strips of silk ribbon are sewn to a woollen cloth base. This appliqué technique is not the same as that employed in Seminole patchwork, as shown in Plate 224. Once well known to most of the Midwestern tribes, garments of such fine condition are rare today, for the silk usually rots rather quickly. This is folded to show the borders.

OSAGE; Oklahoma   L:47 in.   1875–1900
Museum of the American Indian: 2/796

240 *Pipe Bowl*

Portraying a bear and a man struggling for possession of a cask of rum, this fine example of sculpture in small compass is also proof that Indians *do* have a sense of humor.

WYANDOT; Ohio   H:3¼ in.   1775–1825
Museum of the American Indian: 21/3038

241 *Effigy Spoons*

The most common style of wooden spoon for use in large bowls had a curved hook which prevented the spoon from slipping into the liquid. These hooked heads were often carved to represent various life forms. Animals especially were favorite subjects, and usually represented the clan of the owner. The four illustrated here depict a grouse, swan, woodcock, and squirrel.

ONEIDA; Wisconsin   L:8 in. max.   1825–1875
Cranbrook Institute of Science: 2123, 2124, 2125, 2242

242 *Quilled Bark Box*

The technique of working dyed porcupine quills in geometrical designs on a birch-bark base was a major art with this tribe. Early quillwork was dyed in softer vegetable colors; more recently, aniline dyes have been used, as in this example. Sometimes this results in a garish product, but the specimen illustrated is a superior example of the quillworker's art.

MICMAC; Nova Scotia   H:5 in.   1900
Museum of the American Indian: 18/2180

243 *Beaded Pouch*

Heavily beaded pouches are found all through the Eastern Woodlands, extending as far west as the Great Lakes, where they attained their greatest expression among the Chippewa. While they have been somewhat influenced by European shoulder pouches, several indigenous features can be seen. One of the more unusual characteristics is the consistent employment of two entirely differing designs on the shoulder sash. Such imbalanced design refutes the dictum that Indian art is essentially one of bisymmetric layout. This pouch is extraordinary for condition and quality of workmanship as well as for its colorful appearance. Old-time pouches used red-dyed deer hair for the trim; this one employs red yarn.

MOHEGAN;
Norwichtown, Connecticut   Pouch: 9½ × 10 in.; sash: 4 × 20 in.   1850
Museum of the American Indian: 10/9723

244 *Birch-Bark Box*

Birch bark was an important material for the Indians of the northern regions of the United States and Canada, and they used it for a great variety of articles. Decorations on such objects were achieved by scraping away the surface, revealing the contrasting inner bark. This cylindrical box and cover demonstrates that technique. The curvilinear pattern is typical of the eastern Algonquin people, and should be compared with a similar beadwork pattern shown in Plate 243.

PENOBSCOT; Maine   H: 6 in.   1880–1910
Museum of the American Indian: 6/7315

245 *Moose-Hair Pouch*

Made of dyed moose hair sewn onto a black-dyed deerskin base, this fine old piece shows the technique as applied to motifs learned in French convents by young Huron girls. The orange fringe is dyed deer hair. These pouches were used as carrying bags, and are adaptations of early Colonial pouches.

HURON; Canada   Pouch: 8¼ × 9 in.   1775–1825
Museum of the American Indian: 11/5716

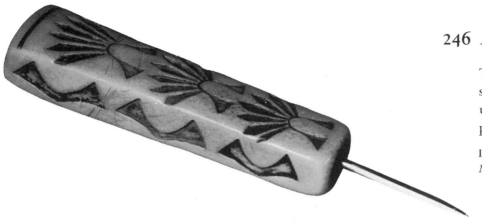

246 *Awl*

The decorative carving on the bone handle of this steel awl shows the Indian tendency to beautify almost everything he used. The original specimen is colored with blue and red pigments rubbed into the incised designs.

Iowa; Oklahoma   L:5 in.   1860–1890
Museum of the American Indian: 12/837

247 *Man's Moccasins*

The moose's hide has many extremely fine hairs which take vegetable dyes readily. Averaging about five inches in length, these were embroidered in various designs on a birch-bark, leather, or cloth base. The technique was used for many centuries to decorate garments and other articles; when Huron girls attended the French-Canadian convents, they were taught European art patterns, which they adapted to their own use. This elaborately worked pair of black-dyed buckskin moccasins shows the art at its very best.

Huron; Québec, Canada   L:9 in.   1830
Museum of the American Indian: 19/6346

248 *Quilled Buckskin Robe*

This is one of the few existing examples of Eastern quillwork which can be dated to the eighteenth century. It was presented to Dr. Samuel L. Mitchell in 1788 by the Seneca in appreciation of his efforts to aid the tribe in legislative matters. While it has been suggested that the robe was used in ancient Otter Society rites, the similarity of the central figures to the Underwater Panthers so common among the Midwestern tribes makes a Great Lakes origin more likely. Presumably it came to the Iroquois in trade. See Plates 227 and 229.

Seneca; New York   33 × 41 in.   1750–1788
Museum of the American Indian: 14/3269

BIBLIOGRAPHY

This bibliography has been compiled on the basis of general availability and thoroughness of illustration, with the purpose of amplifying the present volume. A definite effort has been made to include at least one title for each of the major culture areas and techniques, although thorough coverage of the field is obviously impossible.

Unfortunately, no complete bibliography of Indian art has ever been published, and the present listing does not pretend to fill that gap. Since most of the following titles include individual bibliographies, the interested reader has a rather considerable reference guide at hand.

Those titles marked * will enable the reader to obtain a general introduction to the American Indian and his art. The rest treat the various fields and techniques in a more specialized manner.

ADAIR, JOHN, *The Navajo and Pueblo Silversmiths*. Norman, Oklahoma: University of Oklahoma Press (1944), 220 pp.

ADAM, LEONARD, *Nordwest-Amerikanische Indianerkunst*. Berlin: E. Wasmuth (1923), 44 pp.

ALEXANDER, HARTLEY BURR, *Pueblo Indian Painting*. Nice: C. Szwedzicki (1932), 18 pp. and 50 plates.

AMSDEN, CHARLES AVERY, *Navajo Weaving; Its Technic and History*. Santa Ana, Calif.: The Fine Arts Press (1934), 261 pp.

BARBEAU, MARIUS, *Haida Carvers in Argillite*. Ottawa: National Museum of Canada, Bulletin 139, Anthropological Series No. 38 (1957), 214 pp.

_____ *Haida Myths; Illustrated in Argillite Carvings*. Ottawa: National Museum of Canada, Bulletin 127, Anthropological Series No. 32 (1953), 417 pp.

_____ *Totem Poles*. Ottawa: National Museum of Canada, Bulletin 119, Anthropological Series No. 30 (1930), 2 vols.

_____ *Totem Poles of Gitksan, Upper Skeena River, British Columbia*. Ottawa: National Museum of Canada, Bulletin 61, Anthropological Series No. 12 (1929).

_____ *Totem Poles: A Recent Native Art of the Northwest Coast of America*. Smithsonian Institution, Annual Report for 1931, pp. 559-70.

BARRETT, S. A., *Pomo Indian Basketry*. Berkeley, Calif.: University of California, Publications in American Anthropology and Ethnology, VII No. 3 (1908), pp. 133-309.

BEDINGER, MARGERY, *Navajo Indian Silverwork*. Denver, Colorado: John Van Male (1936), 43 pp.

BOAS, FRANZ, *Decorative Art of the Indians of the North Pacific Coast*. New York: American Museum of Natural History, Bulletin 9 (1897), pp. 123-76.

_____ *The Kwakiutl of Vancouver Island*. New York: American Museum of Natural History, Memoir 8, Part 2 (1905-1909), pp. 307-516.

_____ *Primitive Art*. Instituttet for Sammenlignende Kulturforskning, XIII Series B (1927), 373 pp. Reprint: New York: Dover Publications (1955), 378 pp.

BUNZEL, RUTH L., *The Pueblo Potter*. New York: Columbia University, Contributions to Anthropology, VII (1929), 134 pp.

BURNETT, E. K., *The Spiro Mound Collection in the Museum*. New York: Museum of the American Indian, Contributions, Vol. XIV (1945), 68 pp. and 94 plates.

CHAPMAN, KENNETH M., *The Pottery of Santo Domingo Pueblo*. Santa Fe, N.M.: Laboratory of Anthropology, Memoir I (1939), 192 pp.

_____ *Pueblo Indian Pottery*. Nice: C. Szwedzicki (1933, 1939), 2 vols., 100 plates.

*CHRISTENSEN, ERWIN O., *Primitive Art*. New York: Viking Press (1955), 384 pp.

CODERE, HELEN, *Fighting With Property; A Study of Kwakiutl Potlatching and Warfare, 1792-1930*. New York: J. J. Augustin (1950), 136 pp.

COLLINS, HENRY B., *Prehistoric Art of the Alaskan Eskimo*. Washington: Smithsonian Institution, Miscellaneous Collections 81, No. 14 (1929), 52 pp.

COSGROVE, H. S. and C. B., *The Swarts Ruin; A Typical Mimbres Site in Southwestern New Mexico*. Cambridge, Mass.: Peabody Museum Papers, XV No. 1 (1932), 178 pp. and 236 plates.

*COVARRUBIAS, MIGUEL, *The Eagle, The Jaguar, and the Serpent*. New York: Alfred A. Knopf (1954), 314 pp. and 48 plates.

*CURTIS, E. S., *The North American Indian*. Cambridge, Mass. (1903-1930), 30 vols.

CUSHING, FRANK HAMILTON, *Exploration of Ancient Key Dweller Remains on the Gulf of Florida*. Philadelphia: American Philosophical Society, Proceedings 35 (1897) pp. 329-432.

DAVIS, ROBERT TYLER, *Native Arts of the Pacific Northwest*. Stanford, Calif.: Stanford University Press (1949), 165 pp.

Denver Art Museum, Indian Art leaflet series.

*D'HARCOURT, RAOUL, *Arts de l'Amérique*. Paris (1948).

DIXON, ROLAND B., *Basketry Designs of the Indians of Northern California*. New York: American Museum of Natural History, Bulletin 17, Part I (1902,) pp. 1-32.

DOCKSTADER, FREDERICK J., *The Kachina and the White Man*. Cranbrook Institute of Science, Bulletin No. 35 (1954), 185 pp.

*DOUGLAS, FREDERIC H., and D'HARNONCOURT, RENE, *Indian Art of the United States*. New York: Museum of Modern Art (1941), 219 pp.

DUNN, DOROTHY, *American Indian Painting of the Southwest and Plains Area*. Albuquerque: University of New Mexico Press (1968), 429 pp.

_____ *The Studio of Painting, Santa Fe Indian School*. Santa Fe, N.M.: El Palacio (1960), pp. 1-12.

EARLE, EDWIN, and KENNARD, EDWARD, *Hopi Kachinas*, New York: J. J. Augustin (1938), 40 pp. and 28 plates.

EMMONS, LT. GEORGE T., *The Chilkat Blanket*. New York: American Museum of Natural History, Memoir III (1907), pp. 329-400.

EWERS, JOHN C., *Plains Indian Painting*. Stanford, Calif.: Stanford University Press (1939), 84 pp.

_____ *Blackfeet Crafts*. Washington, D.C.: Office of Indian Affairs (1945), 66 pp.

_____ see under WILDSCHUT, WILLIAM.

*EXPOSITION OF INDIAN TRIBAL ARTS, INC., John Sloan and Oliver LaFarge, eds. (1931), 2 vols., many illustrations.

FENTON, WILLIAM N., *Masked Medicine Societies of the Iroquois*. Washington, D.C.: Smithsonian Institution, Annual Report for 1940, pp. 397-430.

FORBES, ANNE, *A Survey of Current Pueblo Indian Paintings*. Santa Fe, N.M.: El Palacio, Vol. 57, No. 8 (1950), pp. 235-52.

FUNDABURK, EMMA LILA, and FOREMAN, MARY DOUGLASS, *Sun Circles and Human Hands*. Luverne, Alabama (1957), 232 pp.

_____ *Southeastern Indians; Life Portraits*. Luverne, Alabama (1958), 136 pp.

GARFIELD, VIOLA, *The Tsimshian: Their Arts and Music*. New York: J. J. Augustin (1951), 290 pp.

_____ and FORREST, LINN A., *The Wolf and the Raven*. Seattle: University of Washington Press (1948).

GRANT, CAMPBELL, *Rock Art of the American Indian*. New York: Thomas Y. Crowell (1967), 150 pp.

*HARCOURT (D') RAOUL, *Arts de l'Amérique*. Paris: Editions du Chêne (1948).

*HARDING, ANNE, and BOLLING, PATRICIA, *Bibliography of Articles and Papers on North American Indian Art*. Washington, D.C.: Department of the Interior, Indian Arts and Crafts Board (1938), 365 pp. *Mimeographed*.

HAWTHORNE, AUDREY, *Art of the Kwakiutl Indians; and Other Northwest Coast Tribes*. Seattle: University of Washington Press (1967), 410 pp.

HEYE, GEORGE G., *Certain Aboriginal Artifacts from San Miguel Island, California*. New York: Museum of the American Indian, Indian Notes and Monographs, Vol. VII, No. 4 (1921), 211 pp. and 124 plates.

HOFFMAN, WALTER JAMES, *The Graphic Art of the Eskimos*. Washington, D.C.: U.S. National Museum, Annual Report for 1895, pp. 739-968.

HOLMES, WILLIAM HENRY, *Aboriginal Pottery of the Eastern United States*. Washington, D.C.: Bureau of American Ethnology, Annual Report XX (1899), 201 pp. and 177 plates.

_____ *Art in Shell of the Ancient Americans*. Washington, D.C.: Bureau of American Ethnology, Annual Report II (1891), pp. 179-305 and 56 plates.

*HOLMES, WILLIAM HENRY, *Origin and Development of Form and Ornament in Ceramic Art*. Washington, D.C.: Bureau of American Ethnology, Annual Report IV (1886), pp. 437-465 and 25 plates.

INVERARITY, ROBERT BRUCE, *Art of the Northwest Coast Indians*, Berkeley, Calif.: University of California Press (1950), 243 pp.

_____ *Movable Masks and Figures of the North Pacific Coast Indians*. Bloomfield Hills, Mich.: Cranbrook Institute of Science (1941), portfolio.

_____ *Northwest Coast Indian Art*. Seattle: Washington State Museum; Museum Series I (1946).

JACOBSON, OSCAR B., *Kiowa Indian Art*. Nice: C. Szwedzicki (1929), 11 pp. and 30 plates.

*_____ , and D'UCEL, JEANNE, *American Indian Painters*. Nice: C. Szwedzicki (1950), portfolio.

KEITHAHN, EDWARD, *Monuments in Cedar*. Ketchikan, Alaska: Roy Anderson (1945).

*KELEMEN, PAL, *Mediaeval American Art*. New York: Macmillan (1943; 1956), 414 pp. and 308 plates.

KNOBLOCK, BYRON W., *Bannerstones of the North American Indians*. LaGrange, Ind.: The author (1939), 596 pp.

KRAUSE, AUREL, *Die Tlinkit Indianer*. Jena (1888). English edition translated by Erna Gunther. Seattle: University of Washington Press (1956), 310 pp.

*KRIEGER, HERBERT W., *Aspects of Aboriginal Decorative Art in America, Based on Specimens in the U.S. National Museum*. Washington, D.C.: Smithsonian Institution, Annual Report for 1930, pp. 519-56.

*KROEBER, ALFRED LOUIS, *Cultural and Natural Areas of Native North America*. Berkeley, Calif.: University of California, Publications in American Anthropology and Ethnology, Vol. 38 (1939), 242 pp.

*LINTON, RALPH C., *Primitive Art*. Kenyon Review, III (Jan. 1941), pp. 34-51.

LORANT, STEFAN, *The New World: The First Pictures of America*. New York: Duell, Sloan and Pearce (1946), 292 pp.

LYFORD, CARRIE, *Quill and Beadwork of the Western Sioux*. Washington, D.C.: Office of Indian Affairs (1940), 116 pp.

_____ *Iroquois Crafts*. Washington, D.C.: Office of Indian Affairs (1942), 97 pp.

_____ *Ojibwa Crafts*. Washington, D.C.: Office of Indian Affairs (1943), 216 pp.

MALLERY, GARRICK, *Pictographs of the North American Indians*. Washington, D.C.: Bureau of American Ethnology, Annual Report IV (1886), pp. 3-256 and 88 plates.

*_____ *Picture-writing of the American Indians*. Washington, D.C.: Bureau of American Ethnology, Annual Report X (1893), pp. 3-807 and 54 plates.

MARRIOTT, ALICE, *Maria: The Potter of San Ildefonso*. Norman, Okla.: University of Oklahoma Press (1948), 294 pp.

MASON, J. ALDEN, *Eskimo Pictorial Art*. Philadelphia: Museum Journal, XVIII (1927), pp. 248-83.

MASON, OTIS TUFTON, *Aboriginal American Basketry*. Washington, D.C.: U.S. National Museum, Annual Report for 1902, pp. 171-548 and 248 plates.

MERA, HARRY P., *Indian Silverwork of the Southwest, Illustrated*. Globe, Ariz.: Dale S. King (1959), 122 pp.

_____ *Style Trends of Pueblo Pottery in the Rio Grande and Little Colorado Cultural Areas*. Santa Fe, N.M.: Laboratory of Anthropology, Memoir III (1939), 164 pp.

MERA, HARRY P., *The "Rain Bird": A Study in Pueblo Design*. Santa Fe, N.M.: Laboratory of Anthropology, Memoir II (1937), 113 pp.

MILLS, GEORGE, *Navaho Art and Culture*. Colorado Springs: The Taylor Museum (1959), 273 pp.

MOOREHEAD, WARREN K., *Stone Ornaments of the American Indians.* Andover, Mass.: The Andover Press (1917), 448 pp.

*_____ *The Stone Age in North America.* Boston: Houghton Mifflin (1910). 2 vols.

NELSON, EDWARD WILLIAM, *The Eskimo About Bering Strait.* Washington, D.C.: Bureau of American Ethnology, Annual Report XVIII, Part I (1899), pp. 3-518 and 107 plates.

NEWCOMB, FRANC J., and REICHARD, GLADYS A., *Sand Paintings of the Navajo Shooting Chant.* New York: J. J. Augustin (1937), 87 pp. and 35 plates.

NIBLACK, ALBERT P., *The Coast Indians of Southern Alaska and Northern British Columbia.* Washington, D.C.: U.S. National Museum, Report for 1888, pp. 225-386 and 70 plates.

ORCHARD, WILLIAM C., *Beads and Beadwork of the American Indians.* New York: Museum of the American Indian, Contributions Vol. XI (1929), 140 pp. and 31 plates.

_____ *The Technique of Porcupine-quill Decoration Among the North American Indians.* New York: Museum of the American Indian, Contributions, Vol. III, No. 1 (1916), 53 pp.

RAINEY, FROELICH, "Old Eskimo Art," in *Natural History Magazine,* Vol. XL, No. 3 (1937).

RAY, DOROTHY JEAN, *Eskimo Masks, Art and Ceremony.* Seattle: University of Washington Press (1967), 272 pp.

SHETRONE, HENRY CLYDE, *The Mound Builders.* New York: Appleton (1930), 508 pp.

*SIDES, DOROTHY, *Decorative Art of the Southwestern Indians.* Santa Ana, Calif.: The Fine Arts Press (1936), 50 plates.

SINCLAIR, JOHN L., *The Story of Kuaua.* Santa Fe, N.M.: School of American Research, Papers No. 45 (1951), 11 pp.

SMITH, HARLAN I., *An Album of Prehistoric Canadian Art.* Ottawa: National Museum of Canada, Bulletin 37 (1923), 195 pp.

SMITH, WATSON, *Kiva Mural Decorations at Awátovi and Kawaika-a.* Cambridge. Mass.: Peabody Museum Papers, Vol. 37 (1952), 363 pp. and 92 plates.

SNODGRASS, JEAN O., *American Indian Painters; a Biographical Directory.* New York: Museum of the American Indian (1968), 269 pp.

_____ *Decorative Art and Basketry of the Cherokee.* Milwaukee: Milwaukee Public Museum, Bulletin 2 (1920), pp. 53-86.

_____ *Montagnais Art in Birch-bark, a Circumpolar Trait,* New York: Museum of the American Indian, Indian Notes and Monographs, XI No. 2 (1937) 157 pp.

_____ *The Iroquois.* Cranbrook Institute of Science, Bulletin No. 23 (1955), 95 pp.

STEVENSON, MATILDA V., *The Zuñi Indians.* Washington, D.C.: Bureau of American Ethnology, Annual Report XXIII (1902), 634 pp.

STEWARD, JULIAN H., *Petroglyphs of California and Adjoining States.* Berkeley, Calif.: University of California, Publications in American Anthropology and Ethnology, Vol. 24 (1929), pp. 47-238.

_____ *Petroglyphs of the United States.* Washington, D.C.: Smithsonian Institution, Annual Report for 1936, pp. 405-426.

SWANTON, JOHN R., *Contributions to the Ethnology of the Haida.* New York: American Museum of Natural History, Memoir VIII, Part 1 (1905), 300 pp.

*SYDOW, ECKART VON, *Die Kunst der Naturvölker und der Vorzeit.* Berlin (1923).

SPECK, FRANK G., *The Double Curve Motive in Northeastern Algonkin Art.* Ottawa: National Museum of Canada, Memoir No. 42 (1941), 17 pp.

TANNER, CLARA LEE, *Southwest Indian Painting.* Tucson: Arizona Silhouettes (1957), 157 pp.

TOWNSEND, EARL C., JR., *Birdstones of the North American Indians.* Indianapolis: The author (1959), 719 pp.

UNDERHILL, RUTH M., *Pueblo Crafts.* Washington, D.C.: Bureau of Indian Affairs (1944), 145 pp.

*VAILLANT, GEORGE CLAPP, *Indian Arts in North America.* New York: Harper and Brothers (1939), 63 pp. and 96 plates.

WEST, GEORGE, *Tobacco Pipes and Smoking Customs of the American Indians.* Milwaukee, Wisconsin: Milwaukee Public Museum, Bulletin 17 (1934), 2 vols.

WILDSCHUT, WILLIAM, and EWERS, JOHN C., *Crow Indian Broadwerk; A Descriptive and Historical Study.* New York: Museum of the American Indian, Contributions Vol. XVI (1959) 55 pp. and 47 pl.

WINGERT, PAUL S., *American Indian Sculpture.* New York: J. J. Augustin (1949), 144 pp. and 76 plates.

_____ "Tsimshian Sculpture," in: Garfield, Viola, *The Tsimshian: Their Arts and Music,* New York: J. J. Augustin (1951), 290 pp.

WISSLER, CLARK, *Decorative Art of the Sioux Indians.* New York: American Museum of Natural History, Bulletin XVIII, Part 3 (1904), pp. 231-78 and 9 plates.

WOODWARD, ARTHUR, *A Brief History of Navaho Silversmithing.* Flagstaff, Ariz.: Museum of Northern Arizona, Bulletin 14 (1938), 78 pp.